AURORA
BOREALIS

AURORA BOREALIS

CHRISTIAN WITNESS IN ALASKA

ART & CORA GUILLERMO

authorHOUSE®

AuthorHouse™ LLC
1663 Liberty Drive
Bloomington, IN 47403
www.authorhouse.com
Phone: 1-800-839-8640

Published by AuthorHouse   05/12/2014

ISBN: 978-1-4969-0345-7 (sc)
ISBN: 978-1-4969-0357-0 (e)

Library of Congress Control Number: 2014906687

Any people depicted in stock imagery provided by Thinkstock are models,
and such images are being used for illustrative purposes only.
Certain stock imagery © Thinkstock.

This book is printed on acid-free paper.

New Revised Standard Version Bible, copyright © 1989 the Division of
Christian Education of the National Council of the Churches of Christ in the
United States of America. Used by permission. All rights reserved

DEDICATED WITH LOVE

—to Bea Shepard and Claudia Kelsey

who introduced us to the incalculable joy of witnessing

—to Douglas Community United Methodist
Church for loving support of the
ministry.

CONTENTS

PREFACE

In 2005 and 2010 we returned to Douglas, Alaska, for a reminiscent visit and follow up the friends we generated during our work in the Filipino Ministry. Out of these meetings, our friends having witnessed our work suggested that our Christian experience in discipleship should be in written form for the historical archives of modern day witnessing.

Hence this modest volume narrated in the reportorial style of a journalist tells the story of our discipleship as lay people working in the Filipino Ministry at Douglas Community United Methodist Church in Douglas. Our purpose is to share the shimmering highlights of personal evangelism among our country men and women, and record in words and pictures this ministry which we believe has kindled the church community in this picturesque island of Alaska.

Our simple messages in discipleship delivered during our summer visits were specifically designed to reach and awaken our incipient audience of Filipino-Americans. Our messages encapsulate transcendent experience, cultural background and contemporary events. Thanks to the ministers of Douglas. Ketchikan, Anchorage UM churches who graciously shared their pulpits so that we were able to deliver our sermonettes on the Good News of Christ's love and redemption to compatriots. Today there is a impressive presence of Filipino-Americans at Douglas, Ketchikan, and Anchorage Methodist churches among the 28 churches in the Alaska Methodist Conference.

While our epic mission may have ceased, our witnessing still prevails by keeping in touch with most of the people who responded to our discipleship. Our communication rekindles the ember of faith in their struggles of daily living. An inspiring footnote is that several of the children and teen agers, who are mostly grown ups now, have maintained their connection with their churches by their giving, service, and presence. Our ministry of discipleship was the epiphany of our witness for Christ and a transforming episode in our lives. Praise be to God.

The good news radiantly expressed in our messages brightly beams in the last frontier of America.

FOREWORD

Beatrice L. Shepard

When I first met Art he had never been to Alaska. The questions he asked were a lot like those the tourists asked me when they took part in my docent tours at the Alaska State Museum. Most of the people from the part of the U.S. that we Alaskans call "The south 48" seem to think that Alaska is inhabited by Eskimos, or at least the major part of native Americans living in Alaska would be Eskimo. Almost nobody asking questions about native Alaskans would ask about Athabascans, Aleuts, Yupiks, Inuits, Inupiats, Tlingits, or other possible Native groups. I finally explained to Art that I knew very few Eskimos. I told him that almost no Eskimo lived in the part of Alaska where I live. In fact I said, there are many more people from the Philippines living in Juneau area than Eskimo. Art looked as though he thought I didn't know what I was talking about.

"Filipinos in Alaska? Why?"

I gave him a small part of my docent tour—about the fishing industry in Alaska. When the fishing industry organized in SE Alaska, it was soon decided that the best way was to build canneries in Alaska and do the preparation and canning right here. Since this would be mainly seasonal operation, there were very few people available in the area at the time they would be needed to operate the canneries. Soon, it became apparent that, since many Filipinos were coming to the west coast with hopes of staying in America, they might be the answer. In just a few years, the canneries of SE Alaska were being operated each summer with Filipino crews which came at the beginning of the fishing season, and then departed in a body at the end of the season.

It didn't take long before the Filipinos began looking around for possibilities of remaining in SE after the season ended. And, by the time Art and I were talking about it there was a sizable Filipino population in many cities in Alaska.

Much of the Christian work in the Philippines was done originally by the Roman Catholics, but by this time some Protestant groups were operating in the islands, and among them the Methodist denomination stood out. When the Filipinos came to America, they found churches of the denominations they had been attending in the Philippines. Our church, the Douglas Community United Methodist Church in Douglas, Alaska, just three miles from downtown Juneau (capital of Alaska), had twenty or more Filipino members.

When Art asked about Filipinos in Alaska I answered "Come and see." I ultimately convinced him, and he and his wife Corazon came in the summer for a visit. On the Sunday that they visited with us in our church there were some twelve Filipinos present. At the service, Art drew me aside and said, "Here are some things you should do with the Filipinos in your church." When he finished, I said, "I think you are right and I think you are exactly the right person to do them." Art agreed. And the rest is history.

ACKNOWLEDGEMENTS

Funding of the Filipino Ministry work came from the following for which we are eternally grateful: Douglas Community United Methodist Church, First United Methodist Church, Cedar Falls, Iowa (our home church), National Association of Filipino United Methodists. Burns Brodhead of Pennsylvania Conference (Burns was a 1985 ministerial delegate to the General Conference in Baltimore. Art was a lay delegate of Iowa Conference), New Hope Methodist Presbyterian Church, and Advance Specials, and National Association of Filipino-American United Methodists.

We are greatly indebted to the following church members who provided us our housing during our ministry work: Bob & Julie Isaac, LeRoy & Sandra Coon, Johnny & Debra Gerrish, Gerald & Gladys O'brien, Chet & Jean Mattson,

We acknowledge with gratefulness the following Douglas church ministers for their wholehearted support of the Filipino ministry: John & Connie Page, Norvell & Judy Robertson, Kimberly Poole, Ron Covey, and Carol Ann Seckel (Conference Superintendent.)

And many thanks (*salamat po agyaman kami daghan salamat*) to our Filipino and American friends who warmly welcomed us in their homes. **Juneau/Douglas:** Beatrice Shepard & Claudia Kelly. Abad Family (Demetrio & Julia, Jose & Terrie, Ronnie & Marissa, & Wilfredo & Grace), Ampy & Benny Cruz, Rebecca Pintang, Angelita Pintang Carillo, Claudette Curtis, Celestine Aparezuk, Robert & Judith Andree, Rudy Isturis, Claro & Eunice Rodrigo, Mario & Lillian Lim, Danny & Vickie Villanueva, Mike & Linda Taylor, Rick & Julie Sagrado, Loy & Ludy Maturan, Darwin & Marjorie Abad, Salvador & Rosalie Lumba, Freddie Abad, Art & Estrella Floresca, Warlita Mateo, Randy & Wilma Davis, Romeo & Amy Abad. Lorenzo Jarabata Jr, Ponce & Erlinda Agahona, Andres Julotan, Linda Yadao Carillo, Susan Abad, Cora Reece, Carolyn Garcia, Vincent & Femie Yadao, Alfredo Yadao, Larry & Maureen Weeks, Pete & Carlene Bednarowicz, Lenore & Fred Honsinger, John & Lee Sandor. Jim & Ruth Taylor, Verda Cary, Claudette Curtis. Festus & Nwando Nzoiu. **Ketchikan:** Bob & Beverly Bowers, Anastacia Ylanan, Louie & Norma Oposcolo, Godofredo Cabinum, Cecilia & Nilo Leonora, Linda & Amado Montecillo. **Anchorage:** Mel & Jasmine Gallardo, Frank & Clarita Ballon.

A special thank you to my friend Rev. Marvin Ceynar for editorial work and my computer guru Susie Steinbeck for her guidance in the preparation of this book.

FILIPINO MINISTRY IN ALASKA

Aurora Borealis is a kaleidoscope phenomenon of light which often inflames Alaskan skies during summer months and watching it is an unforgettable magical experience of the extraordinary beauty of nature. Our modest story humbly narrated in this book is the Aurora Borealis of our shimmering personal witness for Christ which we would like to share with fellow Christians and pass on to them the transforming messages that we delivered, lessons learned and the visions kindled during our Filipino Ministry work at Douglas Community United Methodist Church during our Filipino Ministry work at Douglas Community United Methodist Church. This congregation is a vibrant body of Christ in the picturesque island of Douglas, Alaska. Douglas church was formed in 1946 when 13 charter members signed the membership book and started worship service in the home of Leigh Grant. A church building was constructed with grants from the Methodist Board of Missions. In the ensuing years as membership grew a larger sanctuary was built in 1952 with intensive labor of love by church members and volunteers from churches representing 23 states. On a clear day the cupola towers over the

Douglas channel and across the bay lies majestic Mt. Juneau. Its strategic location gives the church a religious presence in a bustling community.

The Filipino Ministry work started in the summer of 1992 on the initiative of Beatrice Shepard, iconic historian and lay leader of the Douglas Church, who met Art in 1990 as a fellow member of the General Commission of Archives and History. Armed with the official invitation of the church to start a pilot program of a Filipino ministry, we enthusiastically responded to the challenge as the invitation came at a time Art was retiring from university teaching and Cora was close to retiring from her teaching job as a special education teacher. Our acceptance to start the pioneering ethnic program was not without trepidation in view of our status as lay people and our educational background. But the die was cast and forthwith we went to Alaska for a stint with God in the Filipino Ministry of Douglas CUMC. So for thirteen summer months we were wholeheartedly involved in the outreach ministry (Ministry of the Presence) targeted to reach our compatriots (*kababayans*) with God's marvelous presence and quicken them for active involvement in worship and church outreach programs.

We went to work not only with our hearts and hands but also with our souls. Before we accepted the invitation we were in the Juneau-Douglas area on an earlier invite from Bea Shepard, primarily to assess the potential of a ministry work with the burgeoning population of Filipinos. Through informal random surveys we were able to pinpoint our publics. This is one of the research methods of the successful congregational development program developed by the National Association of Filipino United American United Methodists. We discovered three distinct publics revealed in the survey: (A) middle class, ages 18 to 40, husband and wife work, two or three children, some devout Roman Catholics, some nominals. blue collar workers, many work for the state and federal government. About 75 percent of the Filipinos belong to this cohort. (B) Retired class, ages 45 and above, most receive state and longevity pension, many live with their children (those in Class A). They served as babysitters, "homebodies" to keep the household functioning like cooking, cleaning, and maintenance work. About 20 percent of the Filipino population fall under this category. (C) Mixed class. These are Filipinos married to Americans and native Alaskans (Tlingits, Haidas, Yupiks) and their descendants. These are second and third generations and are proud of their Filipino genetics and heritage. About 5 percent belong to this group.

In terms of language groups, the survey revealed three major categories: (A) Ilocanos, majority group. They come from the Northern provinces of Luzon in the Philippines. Many are old timers, who came to work in the thriving canneries of Alaska in the 30's, and stayed on to develop their own families. Many intermarried with the native Alakans. They are also called Alaskeros (early settlers and pioneers) in Alaska, and some of them married native Alaskans. Hence. their progenies belong to the Mixed Class. In our interviews, we noted that they take pride in their Filipino roots. (B) Bisayans. There are several languages in this category: Cebuanos, Hilagaynons, Waray-warays, and Aklanons/Antiqueños, (C) Tagalogs. Although the Tagalogs are a minority in number, their language Tagalog also called Pilipino is widely used by the other ethnic groups to communicate with each other. Our survey revealed also many other interesting data, such as major family clans (Abads, Carillos and Yadaos). Most Filipinos were employed in state and federal jobs, and their teen age children work for McDonald, Burger King, Subway, and souvenir shops which abound in Juneau.

Since we have identified the potential publics, we zeroed in on the most productive groups. Public number one is the middle class. In the course of our first six months in pursuit of our model in congregational development outlined in the Burning Heart (Visions for Asian-American Missional Congregations) book, the coast was clear where to steer our energies. Interpersonal contacts were made wherever possible with our Filipino brethren. Art's Ilocano FBI background (full blooded Ilocano) and masterful use of the language enabled us to meet many of our *kababayans* on the streets, places of work, fishing docks, grocery stores, and homes. Of course, Cora who is a pure bred Tagalog contributed immensely in opening doors of many homes. Initial contacts were warmly successful as Filipinos are generally hospitable, amiable, and receptive to overtures of goodwill. The usual dialogue in Tagalog or Ilocano is "Kumusta ka. Tiga sanka sa Filipinas." After several initial encounters we developed an operational strategy, which we dubbed as call. visit, invite, and integrate. In other words, we refined our approach by winnowing the "chaff from the grain."

The initial six months of random meetings enabled us to meet some 15 families. In subsequent summer visits, we called and visited some 70 families. Art met the Alaskeros, one of them was Ponce Agahona, a retired chef of the Alaskan Maritime system, who introduced us to more Ilocanos in the community. An off shoot of this ministry was the development of a one-to-one Bible study. He discovered that these old timers didn't know how recite the Lord's prayer in Ilocano. So he taught them the prayer. Subsequent visits led to the Bible study. Several of them have not opened a Bible, much less know the teachings of Jesus. Since Art didn't have an Ilocano Bible, Bea Shepard had to order copies of the *Naimbag a Damag* (Ilocano) and *Banal Na Kasulatan*

(Tagalog) from the Philippine Bible House in Manila. There were also tapes of the four gospels. Their favorite readings are the parables of Jesus. A major lesson that Art impressed on them was the verse John 3.16. Art's class welcomed his twice a week visits as it broke the drudgery of baby sitting rambunctious grandchildren and watching TV, since their children seldom took them out for relaxation. Many held two jobs to support the family and relatives in the Philippines. Graduation time was a moving experience. The five Ilocano Alaskeros were very grateful, and they insisted they pay for the cost of the Bible. Art developed strong connectional friendships with them. Two accepted his invitation to worship at Douglas CUMC.

Since we have been keeping a log on our outreach ministry work, let us share an entry which reflects the warm reception of our kababayans:

"(July 9) Visited Alfredo Yadao in his apartment at South Franklin St, Fred, 75, is one of the Alaskeros and partriarch of the huge Yadao clan. Fred prepared lunch. Dungeness crabs and "papaitan" Ilocano goat stew. Wow. Fred loves to cook. He run a food canteen for the Filipino crew members of the cruise ships. Gave Fred the Ilocano tape of the gospel of Mark. Promised to listen to. While we were pulling out of the parking lot a man approached us and requested if we can bring some of the Filipino crew members to church on Sunday. He saw our van marked "Douglas Community United Methodist Church." The man was David Weltzel, We said "Yes." So Art became a taxi driver hauling some of crew members (Filipinos and Americans) to attend Douglas church. (A job he continued in the subsequent summers of our ministry work)."

Ponce Agahona was my most avid Bible study pupil. He was nearing his 90's but still spright and mentally alert. After our weekly visit he confessed in Ilocano "Art maragsakanac ta nag amam tayo. Addu it naam wak iti pannagadal ko ti Biblia kenca. Apay koma ta bendission naka ni Apo Dios itoy aramid mo kada gitoy Filipino ditoy Juneau." (Art I'm so happy that we have met. I've learned a lot in our Bible studies. May the good lord bless you in your work with the Filipinos in Juneau). We met Ponce while we were doing the survey on the streets of Juneau. Every time we went home he was always at the airport to bid us good bye. He had always a gift. Our price gift was the "Eskimo ulu", which Cora often use in preparing salad at home. At this writing of this memoir, Ponce is now with his Heavenly Father. He knew the Good Shepherd and the Lord's prayer "Ama mi" by heart.

Unfortunately, Art's service came to an abrupt halt one day when he was driving to the hospital to visit a Filipino who was ill with pneumonia. As he was taking a left turn, a another vehicle rammed the church van. Ironically, the other driver was a Filipino and was speeding to beat the red light. Art sustained three cracked ribs and minor injuries on his arms and chest. The van was totaled. Luckily, the accident happened two blocks from Bartlett Hospital. Hospital ambulance immediately salvaged him from the jaws of death. Art was hospitalized for two days. The news of the accident spread out like wildfire that drew many of Art's Filipino friends to visit him. The room was filled with flowers. Cora, who left earlier to catch up with her teaching job, came flying to Juneau to provide consolation as he was alone to carry out our ministry work. By God's grace Art recovered nicely. Douglas church was able to buy a newer vehicle.

Our ministry involved us in several outreach programs of Douglas CUMC. We served as counselors of the elementary camp at the Eagle River United Methodist Camp in Juneau. We had zero experience in youth camping, but our best contribution was the recruitment of kids of the families we had visited. Many were delighted to send their children to the Methodist camp which ran for a week. The structured program of singing, daily devotions, talent night, cabin raids, arts/crafts, and nature hikes appeared to have made them appreciative of the value of camping. Sandie Coon, camp director, saw to it that the activities were fun and meaningful in achieving the objectives of a Christian oriented institution. Luckily, the dreaded black bears decided to absent themselves while we were doing the nature walk. Our noisy entourage probably frightened them. Parents of the Filipino campers brought favorite dishes at the close of camp. One of the parents, a Tlingit whose husband is a Filipino, introduced the "Indian Potlatch" which was a culinary experience for the campers. who also enjoyed the seaweeds, fried hooligan, baked salmon, Indian bread, baked Alaskan dessert. One parent confessed that the camping experience made her two daughters *"mabait na bata"* (good kids)" i.e. obedient and respectful. She wanted to send them to camp next summer. Also that we should be their counselors again. Wow! They also sent them to attend Sunday School at Douglas church. So Art fetched the kids on the church van every Sunday.

One church program with which we were also deeply involved was the annual Vacation Bible School. We served as teachers. Many Filipino children from the Juneau/ Douglas area came to the VBS which ran for a week. One summer the VBS theme was "Wow What an Awesome God!" The kids had a lot of fun learning the program. And on graduation day, the parents attended the closing program where they saw and heard their children's work and participation. The parent's exposure to the VBS school provided an excellent public relations image of our church. They saw pictures of church people at work in the Glory Hole, July 4th annual celebrations, Gastineau School Breakfast Program, and cultural programs. These activities became successful entry points of their interest in the church, since many of them have not experienced a Protestant worship service. Worship attendance at Douglas CUMC was beginning to grow as several families began to attend regularly. To make the service more inclusive we introduced the reading of the scripture in Ilocano and Tagalog read by one of the speakers of the language. Even in Art's sermons, he interspersed his delivery with Ilocano and Tagalog words and phrases to drive his evangelical points. Rhonda Cruz, a talented piano student, joyfully played the hymns and rendered special religious anthems.

A by-product of our involvement in camping was Cora's organization of a children's choir. Although Cora couldn't carry a tune, she recruited the same kids who went to camp to form a choir. With the help of Laurie Clough, church organist, the children' choir provided the anthems for several Sundays. Cora and Sandie Coon went on to start a youth fellowship. Again the kids were the campers and their friends. Cora led the youth in short devotions and followed with fun games. After several Sunday meetings, the group went on to elect officers. When we left for home, the group had enlarged with several more teens who invited more friends and relatives.

We built a wider base of families as we came every summer. Most of them considered us as members of the family and addressed us in the customary honorifics of *tatang* and *nanang*." Thus, we were invited to important junctures of family celebrations like baptisms, weddings, birthdays and simple get-together parties. Our schedule of calling and visitations was booked up. On these occasions Art was often requested to give the opening prayer. In the culture of Filipinos, celebration is a festive occasion where food is in much abundance. After the partying is over, as a custom of Filipino hosts, they usually send their guests with food, we call "pabaon." (to go). Cultural traits never die. Thus, we usually go home with dishes of salmon, pinakbet (Art's favorite Ilocano dish), chicken adobo, lumpia (Cora's dish), and even fresh fish and dungeness crabs. Some celebratory invitations we had to turn down because of conflict with other plans in our tight schedule. In our caring conversations we became impromptu counselors as they sometimes shared their parenting problems, hopes and plans. We comforted them by our patient listening and compassionate prayers. Some of them, especially families with serious behavioral problems were referred to appropriate government agencies community civic organizations.

Another sample on our ministry log is this entry. "(August) Visited Isabelo Bautista, 525 10th St. 70 years old. From Mayantoc, Tarlac. Ilocano. Came to Alaska five years ago. Worked in McDonald. Has an Ilocano Bible given by the Jehovah's Witnesses, while living in Virginia Beach, Va. Interested in reading the Bible. I pointed out my favorite reading Psalm 23. Likes it. Lives with his two sons and two daughters. Sons are employed in the Alaska Maritime service. Expressed a desire to listen to the San Marcos tape with his children." As a sequel the Bautista family was invigorated to attend to their Sunday church service.

Over a brief period the community became aware of our presence as associate workers of Douglas CUMC; hence on many occasions we were invited to community celebrations at the Filipino Community Center. Art was often requested to offer the opening prayer and the Roman Catholic priest gave the closing benediction. Our involvement led us to learn about the internal affairs of the center. The center is the major hang out for fellowship. Its major attraction is the weekly bingo game and major source of income. At that time there was a strong political rivalry for leadership positions in the center. Here's where Art's forte came into play. The president asked me what can I do to clear the toxic atmosphere. Art advised the leaders to implement a public relations program which would project a positive image of a healthy organization, the essence of which is loving cooperation and tolerance. The result was a peaceful election and deepened brotherhood.

The epilogue of this Filipino Ministry came on our twelfth visit. We mentioned to our Filipino families that it's time to integrate them as members of the body of Christ, the church. Thus, on our last Sunday 20 individuals came to the altar and were duly baptized as members of the church. Sponsors included Sandie and Leroy Coon, John Sandor, and Bea Shepherd. It was a joyful and glorious occasion. Thus, we would like to conclude our story with the remarkable words of Rick Warren's transforming book "*The Purpose Driven Life.*"

"Your mission gives your life meaning. William James said, 'The best use of life is to spend it for something that outlasts it.' The truth is, only the kingdom of God is going to last. *Everything* else will eventually vanish. That is why we must live purpose driven lives—lives committed to worship, fellowship, spiritual growth, ministry, and fulfilling our mission on earth. The results of these activities *will* last—forever . . . . There are people on this planet whom *only* you will be able to reach, because of where you live and what God has made you to be. If just one person will be in heaven because of you, your life will have made a difference for eternity . . ."

PICTORIALS OF OUR MINISTRY WORK

Douglas bridge is the main connector of Douglas residents and Juneau. Behind is snowcap Mt. Juneau.

Pastor Ron Covey administering the rite of membership to our Filipino American brethren with Bea Shepard, Cora Guillermo and Sandie & Leroy Coon as sponsors.

Filipino-American members of Douglas CUMC with Pastor Ron Covey. The church holds probably the most members of Filipino-Americans in the Alaska Methodist Conference.

Children at the Vacation Bible School on the closing day and attended by their parents who were delighted in their presentations. Many of these kids attended the church's Sunday School.

Cora enjoyed her Sunday School class. She and Sandie Coon organized the youth group. Art served as the "taxi driver" every Sunday in fetching the children.

Bea Shepard conducting her highly regarded Sunday School class. Bea has been teaching the Sunday School class at Douglas Church for many years.

Bea Shepard and Claudia Kelsey with Johnnie and Debra Gerrish who supported the ministry with follow ups.

Campers at the well-run Eagle River Methodist Camp. Their parents were delighted with the transforming activities of the camp and thankful for the enjoyable experience.

The Eagle River Methodist Camp with members of the Volunteers In Mission team who provided leadership in arts and craft activities. Sandie Coon was the well organized director. VIM teams came from Kansas, Louisiana, Ohio, Michigan, and Iowa.

Ponce Agahona, retired Alaska Maritime chef, was one of the Alaskeros in Art's Bible Study group. His favorite was the Lord's Prayer in Ilocano and loves the Shepherd Song (Psalm 23). He was instrumental in leading Art to meet other Alaskeros, who became avid students of the Bible. He is now with his Lord and Savior.

Vincent Yadao, a 90-year old Ilocano, with wife Femi, Vincent welcomed Art's weekly visit and Bible Study meetings. He enjoyed reading the Bible and memorized the Lord's Prayer. Douglas church gave each student a Bible in their language.

John Sandor presenting certificates of membership to the new members.

July 4th celebration is a crowd drawer annually at Douglas CUMC which serves their famous tasty barbecue, fries, salad, and chips.

Party given by Jose and Terry Abad. Cora holds a delicious dungeness crab.

A 20-lb. Coho salmon caught while fishing on board the boat of Larry and Maureen Weeks in the channel. Catching salmon is at its best in July-August.

Celebration of new members at the church's Grant Hall. Pictured are Claro Rodrigo, Eunice Rodrigo, Marissa Abad, Freddie Abad and Ronnie Abad.

Mario and Lillian Lim and their two daughters Angelica and Nicole. Mario introduced us to a number of Filipino-American families. Mario is the pastor of a vibrant Word of Life Church in Juneau.

Alaska Conference District Superintendent Carol Seckel with Art and Cora. Carol was enthusiastic of the Filipino-American Ministry at Douglas CUMC.

Sandie Coon handing out the Cross & Flame pin to the new members.

Benny and Ampy Cruz and friends attended worship services Douglas UMC. Their daughter Rhonda was the accompanist whenever Art is the guest preacher.

Happy campers. Outdoor hiking amid the forest of pine trees was one of their favorite activity. No bears appeared

Claudia Kelsey and Cora admiring a colorful array of Alaska's flowers. Claudia also produced a book on Alaska flowers and black and white illustrations of winter sceneries which graced their Christmas newsletters.

Her international doll collection is now in a museum in Juneau. See inside back cover of this book for its location.

1

FISHING BY GOSH AND BY GRACE

Matthew 4: 18-22; John 21: 3-12

Matthew tells about the call of Jesus to the first four disciples. These four disciples were fishermen. They were Simon called Peter, his brother Andrew, and the Zebedee brothers, James and John. When Jesus visited with them on the shores of the Sea of Galilee, they were busily engaged in fishing.

A friend from Arkansas who was on a tour of the Holy Land some years ago told me that this species of fish still exists today in the waters of the Sea of Galilee. This fish is now called "Peter's fish," after the disciple. He had a taste of this fish, broiled on the shore, and affirms that it's delicious. Perhaps, but having tasted sockeye salmon, which I've been catching at the hatchery in Juneau, I probably would not exchange Peter's fish for the tasty sockeye.

As you all know, I love fishing. Fishing to me is one of the relaxing sports I have experienced since I came to Alaska. For those of you who are or had been in the teaching profession, sometimes you feel that desire to be away from the confines of a classroom and be out in the open fields or on the windy ocean, and savor the fresh air and crispy spray of the waves.

For those of you who have fished in the bountiful waters of Alaska, I know you understand those thrilling moments when you have a fish on your line struggling to get away with might and fury, while you are endeavoring with equal might to boat this wonderful creature. I couldn't forget the moment in July when I landed my first 25-lb halibut off the coast of Point Retreat. In all my fishing days, this 25 pounder is the biggest I had ever caught. Being a fresh water fisherman in Iowa, the biggest fish I ever caught was a 2-lb large mouth bass.

By gosh, I indeed caught a lunker, but it was by grace I caught it. God in his providence has given me the opportunity to be in this wonderful state of Alaska and fish in its pristine waters.

Jesus started his ministry on the shores of the Galilean sea. Galilee is not a sea, but a large, heart shaped expanse of fresh water lake, about 12.5 miles long by 7 miles wide. There are several towns and villages around the lake. During biblical times, the lake was teeming with fish. The inhabitants on the shore were mostly engaged in fishing for their food and source of income. So there was a thriving fish industry there. To preserve their catch, the fish were salted which were sold and exported. It appears that James and John, the Zebedee brothers, abandoned a profitable business when they left their father and his hired servant to follow the call of Jesus.

Galilee figures largely in the ministry of Jesus because this is where he performed his miracles, such as the miraculous catch of fish by Simon. Jesus told Simon to cast his net on the right side of the boat and netted 153 large fish that the net almost broke with the weight. Capernaum is one of the famous cities on the northwest shore where Jesus lived during part of his ministry. Capernaum is also the hometown of Peter, and it is where Jesus healed the man with the unclean spirit and the paralytic.

When Jesus called the Zebedee brothers to go fishing for men their response was immediate. There was no hesitation, or second guessing, as to the nature of the call. They literally threw caution to the wind and their occupations to follow the Master Fisher. Matthew emphasizes that the Zebedee brothers response was instantaneous.

If Jesus were here today and invites you to go fishing for halibut I wouldn't be surprise with your response. Because of the prospect of catching a big one, I too would respond immediately. But I wonder about your response if Jesus were to ask you to go fishing for men and women. To go fishing for real people. People who are not aware of the Good News, the Good News of Salvation. Jesus called his early disciples to catch men and women to prepare them for the salvation that is to come. I like the account of Luke when Jesus called the brothers to fish for men and women instead of fish in the sea. According to Luke, Jesus said to them: "Don't be afraid from now on you will be catching men."

"Don't be afraid." What an assurance from the Master Fisher. The words are built in guarantee not to be fearful of whatever comes. When I was a growing boy in the Philippines I had always been afraid of the dark. In our boyhood beliefs, night was for creatures of the dark. But my minister father would always assure me not be afraid because he was with me whenever we walk out on the rice fields.

How many of you have been fearful to venture into new experiences, such as a new job, or a new family, or new places. I myself had some reservations about starting the Filipino Ministry even when we accepted the invitation. Our fear was that we had no training in this new venture. Our only experience was in our field of vocation and that is teaching. Cora is a high school teacher. I"m an assistant professor of communications. But the Holy Spirit came to our rescue, and we felt in our hearts the comforting words of Jesus "Don't be afraid."

Why is it that the first disciples were fishermen? And why did Jesus choose these simple, uneducated folks rather than the learned sector of the Hebrew nation.

Jesus recognized one major characteristic of the fishermen. And that is that most fishermen whether they are commercial or sportsmen, have enduring patience. Fish do not bite quickly the moment you throw out your lure or bait. It takes a while, perhaps even hours, before you can even get a nibble. I heard that it takes 60 rod hours to catch a king salmon, 20 hours to catch a halibut. How about fishing for men.

Studies on evangelism reveal that it takes 100 personal contact hours to gain the confidence of persons before they begin to trust you.

"I will make you fishers of men," Jesus said. He is calling us not so much for what we are, as for what he is able to make us, if we are prepared to obey Him.

I grew up in a Methodist parsonage in the Philippines. That should make me a believer in the saving grace of Jesus Christ. But I didn't really catch the Good News until I was 17 years old. It was an American army chaplain who was preaching in a Methodist youth rally who challenged the youth to invite Jesus Christ as their Lord and Savior. A number of us came forward, walked slowly to the altar, bowed our heads, and the preacher blessed us with the words "Jesus is your Lord and Savior. Go into the world with trust and confidence that the Lord will always be with you." Since then Jesus Christ has been with me in all my life, in my college days, with my family and in my profession. He has never failed me.

In the book of Revelation, Jesus is pictured as someone standing outside a door, Jesus calls "I stand at the door and knock If any one hears my voice and opens the door, I will come into his house and eat with him, and he will eat with me."

When Jesus called his disciples to go and fish for men and women, he prepared them by his teachings through the parables, his miracles, healing of the sick, and his preaching. He made it very clear to them who He was and is, the Son of God, sent by God the Father, to take away our sins, which he carried to Calvary and died so that by His resurrection we too can be with Him forever. When the voice of Jesus calls, we should drop everything and respond.

There is a story of a young, brilliant preacher and a 90-year old retired pastor who were guests at a big downtown church in the South. Both of them were requested to say the Shepherd Psalm, Psalm 23. The brilliant preacher recited the Shepherd Psalm 23 with all the eloquence at his command. The people applauded his performance. The old broken down minister, rose weakly from his seat, and started to speak in his gentle voice like he were talking to the Great Shepherd, He spoke from his heart. When he finished, there was silence and a hush fell on the audience. Some tears flowed from the eyes of those who were touched.

The elderly minister knew the Great Shepherd. Do you know the Great Shepherd personally? We must have a first hand experience of this Great Shepherd before we can lead others to his fold.

Three months ago Cora and I came to Douglas by the Grace of God to start this pilot program of the Filipino-American Ministry. We are very grateful for this opportunity to serve in the name of Lord. For these months, we worked with joy and excitement. Meeting fellow Ilocanos, Tagalogs, and Visayans in the community are the highlights of this ministry, We meet them in grocery stores, shopping malls, homes, the hospitals, and places of business. And for me the fun place to meet some of my Ilocano folks is the DIPAC Fish Hatchery, where I have the opportunity to talk to them, even while casting out our lines for that elusive coho salmon.

The objective of this ministry is to reach out to our Filipino-American brothers and sisters, their families, and re-ignite their faith in Jesus Christ. This is the Ministry of the Presence. We bring the Message of Jesus Christ in our personal contacts. By identifying ourselves as members of the Douglas Community United Methodist Church. We do not preach, but rather initiate a conversation about their church life if there's opening for the topic. But the initial contacts are mostly to get acquainted. That's good.

When we lived in Arkansas, Cora and I attended an Evangelism Explosion seminar in the Jonesboro UMC, where our family were members. One of the interesting highlights of the seminar was our approach with our prospective contact. After the initial conversation, the talk starts with a question and this question is quite shocking: The question goes this way: "If you were to die tonight, are you sure you're going to heaven? How do you know you are going to heaven?" Wow! This is what I describe as "street evangelism." I tried this approach once with a fellow Ilocano, as they are approachable and at home when they speak the language. The approach did not work. They are more concerned about the here and now, and not about heaven or hell.

Billy Graham once said the reason we believe in Jesus Christ is not that we could die tonight but that life is so much fuller with Him here and now and were likely to live here and now. That is the Good News.

Well, how do we stock up in our objective of the Ministry of the Presence? We have met some 40 people, and that includes some native Alaskans and whites. We visited some 20 homes. Some of the people are community leaders, but generally we met government employees, mostly Ilocanos, Tagalogs, and Visayans. Some of them are older folks. We have invited some of them to visit the church. We have been successful in inviting their children to attend Eagle River Methodist camp.

An offshoot of my visit with older Filipinos is my tape ministry. These Filipinos are retirees. When I call on these retirees they are generally happy to meet a fellow Ilocano. I give them a tape of the Gospel of Mark in Ilocano. Thanks to be Bea Shepard for this gift, which she ordered from the Philippines. I follow this visit with a one-to-one Bible study. He liked my visit very much. He learned for the first time to say the Lord's Prayer in Ilocano. Since he was a Roman Catholic, he said he never learned the Lord's Prayer in his language. I taught him also the Shepherd Psalm which he loved.

His personal testimony on my last visit was this: "Art I believe in Jesus Christ as my Savior and Lord. Thank you for your visits. I pray every night before I go to bed and ask for God's mercy on my soul. I wish you well in this ministry."

Let me close. The Filipino-American Ministry at Douglas Community UMC is alive and well. There are people in this community who are unchurched and waiting for someone to bring them the Good News. We are only messengers of Jesus Christ who calls us to be fishers of men and women. You and I have a stake in the success of this ministry. Let us again hear the words of the Master Shepherd: "Do not be afraid."

Let us pray.

God Almighty, who through thy son Jesus Christ has called us to be your witnesses, grant us the grace and power to carry your message of hope and salvation to our people in this community. Amen.

2

ENDLESS LINE OF SPLENDOR

Psalm 9: 11-20; Hebrew: 12: 1-6; Peter: 1:1-6

My sermon title "Endless Line of Splendor" comes from the first line of Vachel Lindsay's famous poem, "An Endless Line of Splendor." Bea Shepard in her message two Sundays ago quoted this splendid line. So I decided to use the line for my sermon today. It just happens that I have a copy of the book entitled "Endless Line of Splendor" given by a friend from Nashville, Tennessee.

The book was written by the master story teller of Methodism, Halford Luccock, who died soon after he finished writing the first chapters. Then Webb Garrison took over and added more vignettes to the volume. The book describes the story of our church—The United Methodist Church—of the men and women, their dreams and sacrifices that made the church a power for good and why the United Methodist Church is as strong as ever in spreading holiness in this land and abroad. The book contains gripping stories and anecdotes of men, women, institutions, missionaries, people who devoted their lives, even gave their lives, for the church that you and I may enjoy the blessings of Christ who gives us the power to live and witness for Him.

Let me quote the first line of Vachel Lindsay's poem:
And endless line of splendor,
These troops with heaven for home,
With creeds they go from Scotland,
With incense go from Rome,
These in the name of Jesus,

We are benefactors and inheritors of an endless line of brave souls, daring men and women, pioneers who staked their lives that the church of Jesus Christ may be established in the United States and in all the parts of the world. One of the inspiring stories of the spread of Methodism is in Africa, where today the United Methodist Church is a major religious faith of the majority of African people. I had the pleasure of meeting Bishop Emilio Carvalho of Angola, while we were members of the Commission on Archives and History, and he told me that the Angolan United Methodist Church is a vibrant and growing church. Thanks to the early Methodist missionaries who planted the seeds of the teaching of John Wesley in that country. The Angolans are like us here in United States, they are enveloped by a great cloud of witnesses. These witnesses are those who laid the foundation of this church—its teachings, doctrines, administration, organization, ministers, missionaries, and many other functions that this church may live as the body of Christ on this earth.

I remember my late father, an ordained United Methodist minister, who served the Lord for 45 years in the Philippines. After the end of World War II, there was a call for volunteers to open Methodist work in Mindanao, our last frontier. My father volunteered. He left us in our hometown in Guimba, Nueva Ecija. He served for a year through this difficult period of his ministerial life. He suffered the privation of the frontier settlers—danger of hostility, loneliness, and many other physical problems of the pioneers. But he persevered. Our United Methodist history in the Philippines has credited him for opening preaching points in Cotabato. Today Methodist churches are thriving in that province and in other provinces as well. Where before there was only one Methodist bishop for all the Methodist work in the Philippines, now there are three. And one of them tends to the Methodist work in Mindanao.

When I look back to my father's frontier ministry in Mindanao, I find some comparison with our Filipino American ministry in Alaska. Personal evangelism—talking about the Good News to persons in their homes—is often met with indifference, and some cases a hostile attitude. Cora and I have discovered in our initial survey that the majority of our public are Roman Catholics. Most Filipinos grew up in a tight religious community, where their dominance gave them a bit of an uppity nature over Protestants. So many of them have their opinions and beliefs which are sacrosanct. And so in our visits, we don't broach the subject of religion. Our purpose was to meet and know them. Since we spoke their language we had fun time talking about our background and the joys and trials of living in America.

We spent the summer months getting acquainted with lots of our country-men or *kababayans,* who are so hospitable that we usually get invited to enjoy their special cuisine like paksiw (fish cooked in vinegar and spices), chicken and pork adobo and many other type of delicious dishes. Sometimes, we didn't even have to cook as our visiting schedule includes some families who have invited us for dinner. Our visits subsequently resulted in cultivating an atmosphere of friendship that led us to identify those who are receptive to the Good News.

The initial experience led us to develop an evangelism strategy we gave an acronym—MVI for meet, visit and invite. One cultural trait of a Filipino is friendliness. Say hello or kumusta to Filipino, and you always get a friendly smile and sometimes friendly chat. That is the opening gambit for us to engage in a casual meeting. Then in subsequent meetings, be on the street or places of work, we get an invitation to visit their home, or we may also initiate a visit to our apartment. Filipinos welcome reciprocity in social invitations. That's one cultural trait that Filipinos have carried on in their adopted home land-the United States. So, in the course of our visit with those who have welcomed us we begun to establish a closer relationship.

One of the inspiring examples of this strategy was the response we got from a couple whom we met through another newly cultivated friend. This couple, who had two beautiful daughters. We classified them as "unchurched" or nominal Roman Catholics. After several visits, we mentioned about visiting our church worship service on Sundays. Their response was enthusiastic. They liked the services. And, they even sent their daughters to attend Sunday School. Thus, I started a van service to pick up their daughters and other people to attend Sunday School. And soon many of the other Filipino kids joined the girls to attend the Eagle River Methodist camp in Juneau, AK where we served as counselors. Our witness began to blossom.

An offshoot of our visits with several families as we begun to know them better and learned of their problems, joys, successes, worries, ailments and so forth. Thus, we became impromptu counselors. Our teaching background was valuable. Our counsel, advice, and words of comfort were always welcome. And they thanked us profusely for opening their minds, providing new perspective and strengthening their faith.

For the past months, we have been attending the adult Sunday School class of Bea Shepard and Sheryl Cole. We use a book entitled "God is not Finished with Us Yet." The book is about the major promises of the minor prophets such as Hosea, Amos, Micah, Jonah and Nahum. Although the message of these prophets were addressed to the Israelites thousands of years ago, there is a contemporary ring to us people of the 21st Century. These prophets are talking about social justice, peace, reformation, the coming reign of God and judgment. These minor prophets are speaking to us today, calling us to repentance, acknowledge our sin, face up to our past and experience God's forgiveness.

The God of history is working with us in all our waking and sleeping hours. He is standing at the door of our hearts, knocking so we can let Him in, and enthrone Him in our soul.

There is an inspiring story about Senator Harold Hughes from Iowa. He was a senator in the early 70's. He is the only senator who left the senate to enter full time religious work. This one-time truck driver and alcoholic was so transformed by a conversion experience that he threw away his bottle one night and declared "the nation is my parish." He met Jesus Christ in 1954 in a

Methodist evangelistic rally in Iowa. Thus, he resigned his senate seat and devoted the rest of his life telling what God has done for him and what Christ can do for them too.

I wonder how many of you have read the book of Bea Shepard and Claudia Kelsey "Have Gospel Tent Will Travel." This book is a testimony in words and pictures of people who devoted their lives and fortunes to make what the Alaska Missionary Conference is today. This is a book that chronicles 160 years of Methodist history in Alaska, What this book tells us is the endless line of splendor that was opened up by these pioneers of the faith and that we the inheritors should keep this faith moving forward with our witness and God's infinite blessings.

I'd like to close with this ancient story. There is an old beggar who begged for rice at the city gates every day. He cried "Alms, Alms" to every passerby. One day a Prince passed by and the beggar called "Alms, Alms." The Prince heard the beggar and dismounted. He asked the beggar "What have you to give me for the alms I might give you?" The beggar fingered three grains from his bag and gave it to the Prince. The Prince took the three grains of rice and put them back into the beggar's hand and carefully folded his hands. The Prince left the beggar and entered the city. As the beggar walked back, he opened his hand. To his amazement there lay three brilliant diamonds. He gasped and wept. "If only I had given all."

Let's pray.

All mighty and ever loving God, we thank thee for the witness of our missionaries who opened the way for us to follow in their footsteps. Grant to us the courage to carry on the work of sharing your love and mercy with our country men in this community. Amen.

3

BREAD OF LIFE

Matt.4:3-4; Luke 22.19

As you all know bread is the staple food in the Western world. It is the stuff of life. It is the basic food for those who live in the temperate zone. But for most of us who grew up in the tropical zone and the eastern side of the globe, our grain of life is rice.

In the Philippines, where I spent the better part of my life, rice is the staple at every meal. Bread to us is an item for the merienda, that is, served as a snack. It is not the main meal item. When rice is harvested there is great rejoicing and celebration in the provinces. A shortage of rice means hunger and suffering. Rice has definite political value. People blame the government for the shortage. Of course, shortages are not the government's fault as it is often due to natural calamities such as typhoons and floods. So rice is often imported from Thailand which produces a surplus of the commodity.

I remember as a boy during the Japanese occupation of the Philippines in 1943-1945. We had to subsist on rice gruel, a very thin rice soup which does stay long in the stomach. The Japanese army had commandeered our rice supplies. Our hunger was alleviated by the timely arrival of the liberating American forces of General Douglas MacArthur. With them came the famous California rice. To us Filipinos, California rice was heaven sent. No longer did we go to bed with hunger pangs.

Bread as mentioned in our scripture reference not only refers to the material element which sustains life, but especially to its spiritual aspects. This has come very vividly in our work in the Filipino-American Ministry in the Juneau-Douglas area. The ministry is bringing the "bread of life" to our Filipino brethren, we call kababayans. There is a crying hunger for spreading the word of God, the story of Jesus and His gift of salvation.

In the past three months in our ministry work, we have visited with some 20 Filipino families in the area. Ninety-five percent of these families are engaged in the pursuit of making a living. They are employed in the government, private business, and maritime jobs. We found some of the bread winners are involved in two jobs. Yes, they are all pursuing the American dream—a house, car, fishing boat and most of the material things that make for comfortable living. Sad to say, they apparently neglected Jesus' admonition, that "man shall not live by bread alone, but needs every word that God speaks."

Some of our Filipino friends have very little time in their work schedule to attend to the spiritual aspects of life. Like many of those we met, church is the time to attend to baptisms, weddings, and certain feast days in their church. There is too little time in these experiences to lift the spirit and feed the soul.

The temptation to work yourselves to the limit is overwhelming. The workplace rewards those with energy and ambition. That's well and good. That is the American spirit as well as the Filipino spirit. Work hard for the material rewards are good. But of course there is a price to be paid. Family life is sacrificed for the almighty dollar. Health is jeopardized. Most of all, the spiritual life withers like a tree that is deprived of the nutrients for the soul. Filipinos are not alone in our mixed up priorities. Our white brethren are in it, too.

As the Bible says: "For what shall it profit a man, if he gains the whole world and loses his own soul."

But there is good news in our ministry. In our many visitations, we found that the elderly and the retirees have the time to listen during our visits. In fact, they welcome us when we call on them. Why, because they have the time. They like to talk to us who speak their language. In many cases, we become like long lost friends. There are many things to discuss in our caring conversations.

In our ministry, I use a tape in Ilocano on the Gospel of St. Mark to conduct a one-to-one Bible study. We run the tape and follow the text with a Xerox copy in Ilocano of the gospel. While we go through verse by verse, I add explanations and background on some difficult passages. We don't discuss the theological and high-faluting aspects of the verses. We talk about the practical or pragmatic application of the verses in their lives. They enjoy the parables of Jesus, for these stories have a clear point, moral lessons which have relevance in their lives.

One of the heartwarming experiences with my elderly folks is that many of them, for the first time, have learned the Lord's prayer. For Roman Catholics they are not taught the Lord's Prayer, at least to those we've have ministered to. So when they memorized the prayer in their own language, they feel uplifted and thank me for teaching them the word of God. For most of us who grew up in a Protestant household, reciting the Lord's prayer is a given. It is embedded in our psyche and soul.

It addition, I taught them also the Shepherd Psalm, i.e. Psalm 23. The Shepherd Psalm in Ilocano is pure poetry and the reassuring tone gives them unlimited hope. They like that part of the Psalm which says: "Though I walk through the valley of the shadow of death I shall not fear, for thou art with me." As a graduation gift I give my senior citizen students a Bible, courtesy of the Douglas Community United Methodist Church.

The divine encounter with our Filipino kababayans continues. Today, we gather at the Lord's table to break bread. We do this in remembrance of the great sacrifice of our Lord Jesus Christ, who gave his life, his body, and blood for the remission of our sins. He took our sins away so that you and I are worthy of the gift of salvation. Jesus Christ instituted this sacrament of Holy Communion to remind us that the bread and wine are the symbols of his body and blood which was shed for you and me.

The Lord invites you to come His table,

4

SENDING OUR MESSAGE

Matt. 28: 16-20; Hebrews 12: 1-3

Let me begin my message this morning with a story that is relevant to my sermon title "Sending our Message."

There was a certain mother who was becoming very anxious over her daughter's failure to bring her boy friend to church to worship God. One day, the daughter told her mother that a handsome young man who seems interested in her would be calling. The first thing her mother asked was "What is his religion?"

The daughter replied: "Mother, I'm afraid he doesn't go to any church. He's an agnostic. So what do you want me to do?

The Mother advised: "You have to sell him your faith in God,"

"Ok, Mom, I'll give it my best shot," said the daughter.

Then came the first date. "How did it go?" asked the anxious Mother.

"Beautiful, Mom," the daughter replied. "I sold him on the blessed Trinity."

The mother was elated. After the second date, the daughter reported she had sold him on the importance of the Holy Communion."

Finally, when it seems that the happy ending was at hand, the girl came home totally distraught and heartbroken.

"What happened?" asked the worried mother.

"I oversold him," she replied. "Now he wants to be a priest."

In our gospel lesson today, Jesus said, "Go therefore and make disciples of all nations. Baptize them in the name of the Father, the Son, and the Holy Spirit. Teach them to carry out everything I have commanded you."

What does this mean for us? Let me pick up the active verb in the sentence. "Go into all the world and preach the gospel." Go is our marching order as Christians. We must go to the community, ghettos, towns and so forth. Go was the marching order of Methodist circuit riders, who spread the seeds of Methodism in the Eastern and Western frontiers, Go was the marching order of the pioneers who planted the seeds of the Wesleyan doctrine in the prairies.

Then the other active verb is *make* as in "Make disciples of all nations. The implication here is that we must do something. That is. we must send our message of love, hope, and enduring faith to our community. Bring the Good News for those who have not heard it. That was what the early American Methodist missionaries shared in the Philippines.

Much is being said today about the mission of the church. The mission of the church is being eroded by signs of decay, such as alcoholism, drug, infidelities, divorces, budget shortages, congregational closures, and so forth. Name me a church in this community that is not faced with these issues and problems. The United Methodist Church is a great institution, but it is not without short coming. Church statistics reveal that our membership roster has declined significantly, and continues to do so, despite massive efforts of our episcopal leaders, program agencies to stem the tide of accretion and introduce transforming ventures.

But we are not alone in this loss of membership. It's happening to all the mainline churches, including the great Roman Catholic Church. In Iowa, there are several dioceses that have already closed because of membership and clergy loss.

But for us United Methodists, the future is not so bleak. We don't thrive on misery. In the last twenty years new ethnic churches have sprouted in urban areas, such as Korean, Vietnamese, Hmong, and Filipino. Hispanic Methodist churches have opened up in California and Texas. There is an increased enrollment of seminary students in Methodist theological schools. And further good news is that our membership decline has leveled off.

But still the question remains, why are we losing members? Where did these people go, or why are we not keeping up with population growth? The US has increased population by 25 percent in the last ten years. Survey after survey show that there are many unchurched people in the nation, in big cities and larger urban areas. Hence, you notice the growth of mega churches in St. Louis, Los Angeles, and Dallas, to mention a few.

In our layman's point of view, we would say that the problem is largely due to our becoming more church centered and not Christ-centered to use a Wesleyan tenet. We are interested in maintaining the administrative structure of the church with so many agencies and program boards that are doing overlapping activities. We need to focus our message on what we do best as Methodists: preach Christ and spread His holiness. Isn't this the message of the pioneers of our faith who spread Methodism like wild fire in the prairies and the west in this nation? From what we hear today from our pastors and episcopal leaders is that their messages have become liberal and socially oriented and emphatic spiritual gratification. Hence, our young people are being bombarded by quick fix messages of instant hope and faith by glib preachers on television.

As most of us know, the youth of our church are the church of tomorrow. If we lose our young people by not attending to their needs then tomorrow is lost in the shuffle. In our church in Cedar Falls, Iowa, we have a full time youth director who has led programs, projects, and services that are designed to keep and maintain their interest and loyalty in the church. We have a contemporary worship service filled with contemporary music and messages of the Good News. Our four girls grew up in this church, and the end result is that now they have their own families who have kept their church connection.

Those of you who might have read David Downing's book *The Most Reluctant Convert,* may remember the faith journey of C.S. Lewis. Downing quotes Lewis as saying: "I have passed on from believing in God to definitely believing in Christ, in Christianity." He added that "the life of a Christian is difficult."

Yes, I submit that life as a Christian is hazardous. We are experiencing confusion, restlessness, joblessness, emptiness, anxiety, loneliness, and alienation. It is true that we live in a very complicated and complex world. Advanced technology. modern science, amazing computers and instant mass communication have changed our world and affected our way of thinking, Pick up any daily newspaper, and you'll read a lot of information of conflict, violence, and catastrophes. As we say in journalism, no news is good news. I'd like to reverse that statement. Good news is no news.

In the midst of all these trouble some environment, is there any message of hope, good news? My answer would be an unqualified Yes, a booming yes! As the scripture says: "All things are possible to him that believes." My heart and soul believes in this divine promise. We must believe that we are delivering the Good News of salvation in Jesus Christ. We must believe that our message and witness are making an impact in our daily contact in our community and neighborhood.

As Marshall McCluhan, the guru of mass communication, said: "The medium is the message." We are the medium by which the message is delivered to our people.

I was fishing at the hatchery yesterday, and I saw a fellow fisherman catching coho salmon every time he casts his silver lure. I told him I'm also using the same kind of silver lure, but I was not pulling a salmon as well as he does. He commented: "You must believe in your lure. You must have confidence that your lure will catch." He made his point. We must have the confidence in our message that Christ is with us in our delivery.

We must believe that God's power through Jesus Christ is great enough to bring forgiveness, healing, comfort, peace of mind, new life and new hope. We need to let people know that there is hope in their lives.

For does not the Bible say: "For God so loved us that He gave his only begotten son, Jesus Christ, that whosoever believes in Him shall not perish but have everlasting life." That's the good news of our message.

The New Testament church was blessed with great preachers like, Paul, Barnabas, Apollo, and others. The fact is that Christianity spread like wild fire over the vast Roman empire, not due so much to their great preaching but to the testimony and witness of ordinary people who went out to tell their friends and neighbors about the amazing Christ whom they knew, and how this Christ had transformed their humdrum lives.

Christianity is a religion of change, and unless what is happening in this church is changing us into more loving and caring persons, changing our attitude, and behavior, I fear we are not really listening and living the Word of God. We can talk the talk and walk the walk about our Christian faith to the community, but we'll accomplish nothing if we remain unchanged and not transformed. We cannot challenge our community unless we ourselves give evidence of having been transformed by the Gospel of Jesus Christ.

We cannot love other people, unless we love ourselves. In the book of Acts, we find that the distinguishing mark of a Christian; "Behold how these people who call themselves as Christian love one another!" Love is their outstanding mark. Can people in our community say to us: "Look how those people who call themselves Methodists love one another?"

By our love, our service, by our gifts, by our abilities, we are sending our message to the community about the Good News of Jesus Christ.

Let's pray.

"I pray that your love will keep on growing more, together with true knowledge and perfect judgement, so that you will be able to choose what is best . . . Your lives will be filled with the truly good qualities which only Jesus Christ can produce, for the glory and praise of God" (Phil. 1: 9-11. TEV) Amen.

Note: Bible verses in my messages are mostly taken from New Revised Standard Version (NRSV), and others are from the Living Bible (LB), and Good News Bible (TEV).

5

RUNNING THE RACE FOR GOD

2 Timothy 4: 7-8

Good Morning. As you all know a minister I am not. My academic training is in communication, journalism and public relations. My message this morning "Running a Race for God" comes from my life experience. I'm not a runner. This running is about a race for God. In Ilocano, it roughly translate as "Iti Lumba Para Ken Apo Dios."

Running, jogging, and exercising has become a fad nowadays. Walking has become a daily routine for the health conscious. That is well and good for the body and mind. We run, jog, or walk to improve our cardio-vascular system or lower our blood pressure, or control our glucose level. We also do these exercises to burn unneeded calories in our bodies.

Cora and I do our walking around our neighborhood in good weather and around the mall in winter. By so doing we notice that our blood pressure has gone down, my glucose level has been controlled, and our cardio-vascular circulation has also improved. We have a very good Egyptian doctor who is caring and kind.

As many of you know President George W. Bush has just started a national physical fitness program, and he showed us that he is a running president. We often see him racing with his aides around the White House. He wants to be physically fit to run the vast affairs of the government. He has also paid attention to his spiritual health as we see him and Laura often go church. He also often invoked the Almighty for spiritual guidance and ends his messages sometimes with God bless America.

Now in running a race for God, we are involved in a spiritual mind set. That is we make a personal covenant with God that we will run in the race with all our heart and soul. And in this race God has set the parameters or markers for us.

The first step in this spiritual race is to run with a **purpose**. We are all together on a spiritual race for God. We are all engaged in a race for our lives with God to reach a goal. In this race there are losers and winners. Those who fall by the wayside, and those who reach the finish line. So if we will be winners we need training in this race and know the purpose of our training. The purpose is already set for us by St. Paul in his letter to the Philippians 3:12-14. He says "Not that I have already obtained all this, or have already been made perfect, but I pressing on to take hold of that which Christ Jesus took hold of me. Brothers I do not consider myself yet to have taken hold of it. But one thing I do is: Forgetting what is behind and straining toward what is ahead, I press on toward the goal to win the prize for which God has called me heavenward for Christ Jesus."

In other words, St. Paul tells us that in a race we must press on, give our best, and forget what is past, not to look behind, and keep our mind, focus, on Jesus Christ. That is our purpose. In a race we must concentrate on what is ahead, not to be side track, with who is behind us. If you have seen Pikabo Street in the recent Olympic Winter Games she looked straight ahead. She didn't look behind, or sideways, but skied with all her might to reach the finish line. She didn't win the gold, but she gave her best shot. She reached the finish line.

When I was a boy my father taught me how to ride a bicycle. When I mounted the bike, while he held the frame, he said: "Look straight ahead. Do not look back, sideways or front wise. Keep pedaling forward slowly." Likewise in this race for God our mind and heart should be clear that straight ahead is the crown of victory which awaits us. We cannot undo the past, the mistakes, errors but we can do something about today and tomorrow.

That is exactly what St. Paul is telling us that in our race for God we should look ahead and run with purpose.

If we run with a purpose we know where we are going. We want to be spiritually fit just as we want our bodies to be physically fit to meet the rigors of our journey of faith.

The second marker is **perseverance** in our race for God. If we are to survive, we must not only run with a purpose, but also run with perseverance. In the athletic world this means we have to have endurance. Likewise, in the spiritual race for God we have to have perseverance. In plain language we must have staying power. The will to stay in the race. Once you are in this race for God you can't quit. Once the shot is fired, you sprint. No turning back.

Let me give an example. Lance Armstrong, the three-time champion of the Tour de France bike race. This Sunday is the final lap of the race. Last year he practiced and practiced with his team mates. Armstrong's forte was biking through high mountain passes. He developed his stamina in the final phase and when the test came on those tight mountain roads he came through with flying colors. He won with the support of his team mates. He carried the flag of his team to the finish line. Athletes are the best examples when it comes to endurance. Players win games with perseverance and endurance. Likewise, in our spiritual quest for God we must have the perseverance to win the race.

As you can see we are not alone in this race. We have the support of a "great cloud of witnesses," those who have successfully run the race. Winners in a race run successfully because they have the support of teammates and coaches. As we run this race, we have our cloud of witnesses, cheering us with their prayers so that we reach the finish line. I'm sure that my late father and mother who are now in heaven were cheering me on to persevere in this race so that someday I may stand with them in the line of victory. I'm sure that all of you have your cloud of witnesses praying for you that you will reach the finish line.

In Galatians 6: 9, St. Paul says: "Let us not lose heart in doing good, for in due time we shall reap if we do not weary." That's perseverance.

The markers are set on the road as our guide to lead us to God. And to follow these markers, St. Paul clearly admonishes us that we must lay aside every weight and sin that clings closely and let us run with perseverance.

Perseverance means that we must also be steadfast (1 Cor. 15: 58). We must be firm. Again St. Paul says, "My dear brothers and sisters, stand firm and steady. Keep busy always in your work for the Lord, since you know that nothing you do in the Lord's service is ever never useless."

So many start the race like a lightning flash-shot, fast and dazzling, encouraged by hot shot TV evangelists.

And some grow weary and fall in love with the world pulled by the blandishments of a materialist society. What happens along the way that swells the ranks of quitters and few finishers. I really wish I knew the answers. If I did I'd shout from this pulpit, or whisper to every discouraged person I meet before it is too late.

Finally in this race for God, we must run with the **power** that God gives us. Athletes prepare their bodies by eating nutritious food and avoiding detrimental substances. Likewise, we must attend to our spiritual diet. I get my spiritual nourishment by coming to church to worship God in the company of believers. Some people claim that they can worship God in the wilderness, in the office, in their fishing boats, or wherever they are. But for me there is no substitute for an organized corporate worship of God in His sanctuary. It is here in this sanctuary of God, in the company of believers that I derive the power I need in my race for the prize for which God has called us heavenward in Christ Jesus.

We come to church to recharge the power we need in the race for God. Like the batteries in our cars the power is drained and used up in our constant starts every time we drive the car. This is the same way with our spiritual batteries. The power is used up in our daily grind for a living. Every day we face the strains and challenges of our vocations. Then our energies are exhausted. We need the nourishment that comes from Christ who is our main source of our strength. In company with fellow believers, we come to church to be involved in prayers, singing and fellowship. And most re-charging of all these involvement is the sermon of our pastor whose training and experience in running a house of worship further push us closer to the finish line. The Holy Communion which we have once a month connects us to the mystical blood and body of Christ. By these symbolic elements we are directly charged to our power base. Jesus says (John 15: 4): "Remain in union in me, and I will remain in union with you. Unless you remain in me you cannot bear fruit, just as a branch cannot bear fruit unless it remains in the vine."

Men of faith are my favorite examples of spiritual power, because they remained connected to God to the end. Frank Laubach, the famous missionary to the Muslims in the Philippines, is an example of a man of enduring faith. I had the privilege of meeting this man of God in Syracuse when I was studying at Syracuse University. Laubach is famous for developing the "each one teach one" method of reading and writing to people in Mindanao. As a result, many Muslims were able to read and write in their language. He didn't convert any Muslim to the Christian faith, but he remained true to his commitment to run the race for God. He served God as a Christian missionary not only in the Philippines, but also to other countries teaching people how to read and write in their own language.

In this race we are running against time. Many people would say: there is plenty of time to do this or that. You don't worry. But we do not realize that we are racing against time. Time is not in our hands. Time is in God's hand. Our race is a divine appointment. When God calls us we must be ready. What a blessing to say in the words of St Paul: "I have done my best in the race, I have run the full distance, I have kept the faith." And now the prize of victory is waiting for me, the crown of righteousness which the Lord, the righteous judge, will give me on that Day, not only me, but to all of those who wait with love for Him to appear."

Let's pray:

Almighty and ever loving God, source of all our strength, give us the will that wearies not and fails not, so we can run the race for thee with power and receive the crown of victory. Amen

6

THE SHEPHERD'S SONG

Psalm 23

Good Morning. I'd like to share with you my modest reflections on one of the most beautiful verses in the Bible. That is Psalm 23 also called the Song of the Shepherd. Psalm 23 is one of the 73 psalms probably written by David in the Old Testament. Some experts believe that certain psalms were written by others but honored David using his name. Thus, the psalms are attributed to be the songs and prayers of David as he poured his heart and soul to God in joy, despair, hope, and thanksgiving. The psalms are the most familiar and best loved portions of the Old Testament.

They are regularly used in Jewish and Christian worship, both as songs and responsive readings. Did you know that the Muslims consider the psalms as one of their sacred books alongside the Koran? When I called up two of my minister friends in California and Kansas and asked for their thoughts about Psalm 23, they replied that they do not use Psalm 23 in preaching, except in a funeral.

Well, I told them I was preaching before a live congregation. They said: "Good luck." And so here I am today taking up the cudgels for Psalm 23 as my main message. I did some research on this famous song of David.

For a starter, I noticed the verses projects a rhythm of beauty, a comforting feeling, and a powerful reassurance of God's majestic and everlasting love. Although the psalms are considered poetry, they don't rhyme. In those days songs were written for the ideas and language. Years ago, I really didn't catch the significance and impact of Psalm 23 until one of my friends said that reading and hearing the Song of the Shepherd in Visayan language was so wonderful, so gripping and enthralling that his soul soars with David. My friend is now with that Good Shepherd, whom he loved and adored.

As I looked to my life I have discovered the truth, comfort, and reassurance embedded in the Song of the Shepherd.

In our moments of despair and grief as the remembrance of the passing of our dear beloved daughter Lualhati sweeps through our hearts and soul, Cora and I turn to Psalm 23 for comfort and consolation. We recite Psalm 23 silently in our hearts to reassure us over and over that our daughter is now with the Good

Shepherd who has been with her all her life and now resting happily in those green pastures and still waters. She has entered the sanctuary of God.

As we reach the threshold of life described as growing old we begin to realize that there are certain things in the Bible we take for granted. What I mean is that some verses and passages become cliches and humdrum, worn out words which have lost their meanings because glib preachers on radio and TV often quote verses in the scripture without feeling for their meaning and sense. Thus, it often seems that their frequent use of familiar verses leads us to believe that they have lost their relevance and application in our lives.

That is why it is good to read another version of the Bible and thereby gain a new perspective of verses to become acquainted again with the ways and thoughts of God. So this morning I'd like to clear up a cliche and share with you what the Shepherd Psalm means to me. I'll go with you verse by verse of the Shepherd Psalm using three sources. These are the Living Bible (LB), Good News Bible (GNB), and the New Revised Standard Version (NRSV) and the Complete Psalms (CP).

There are approximately 110 words in these six verses. Each verse is loaded with affirmations and thoughts of God's love. By reading and listening to them again from a different perspective this can renew and refresh your hearts and understanding on what it means to follow the Good Shepherd.

I'll read the verse in the Living Bible and the Good News versions.

Verse 1: "The Lord is my shepherd I have everything I need." (GNB and LB)

"The Lord is my shepherd I have everything I want." (New RSV)

"The Lord is my shepherd, there is nothing I want." (CP)

David uses the image of the shepherd as the Lord God who is addressed as Yahweh by the Hebrews. The shepherd is a concrete figure with whom the Hebrews could easily identify. And for us Filipinos we call our minister "pastor." Pastor of the flock. Isn't that great? I'm always proud to be called "son of the pastor." We have a great respect for our pastor. So to call God as shepherd makes that identification clear as the provider of all our needs and wants. The "pastor" is also the protector, who defends the flock from any predator such as wolves, which were plenty in the Palestine of Old Testament times.

In describing the Lord as a shepherd, David was expressing his own experience. He spent his early years caring for sheep. Each morning David sounds his horn to call the sheep. The flock rises up to follow the Master to the feeding ground to grassy meadows and sheltering pool. The Good Shepherd never left his sheep alone. The sheep would be lost in the vast meadows and hills in ancient Palestine. His presence was then assured of their safety from predators and comfort in their feeding. The sheep is a docile and sometimes dumb animal and ready to surrender in the face of danger.

That is the kind of image I see the Lord as provider of our needs and wants, and a protector against danger that we face everyday. I saw the reality of this image in my life as one raised in the parsonage. My father was a minister and my mother was a deaconess. Both of them worked as a team. There were five of us children. Inspite of our slim resources, the Good Shepherd had provided us the wherewithal of living, protected and guided us through all our lives. My parents had fully trusted the Good Shepherd. And they are safely in the eternal fold of the Good Shepherd.

The New Testament calls Jesus the Good Shepherd (John 10: 10). Jesus says: "I am the Good Shepherd. The Good Shepherd lays down his life for the sheep." Yes, Jesus laid down his life for our sake when he died on Calvary so that we who believed in Him shall live with Him forever. I would not be standing before you today if I didn't believe that the Good Shepherd has led me all my life, and that I have His assurance of a place in His heavenly kingdom.

Verses 2 & 3. "He lets me rest in the meadow grass and leads me by the quiet streams. He restores my failing health. He helps me do what honors him the most." (LB)

"He lets me rest in the fields of green grass and leads me to quiet pools of fresh water. He gives me new strength. He guides me in the right paths as he has promised." (GNB)

"You guide me toward tranquil waters, reviving my soul. You lead me down the paths of righteousness, for that is your way." (CP)

Our Shepherd directs us to the green grass, peaceful waters and the right paths. We don't know where these places are, but if we let him lead us we will find these places, not literally, for these are symbolisms for contentment, happiness, and peace of mind. Our souls are refreshed and gain new powers to continue on our journey of life. These meadow grasses and still waters are not often there when we need them. Like lost sheep, we will not find provision and protection on our own. But by being a member of the flock, the Lord will not allow, not even one person to go astray, because He knows us.

The ancient Good Shepherd knew their sheep by name. He was acquainted with all of their ways, peculiarities, and characteristic marks. In the same way, this Shepherd, our God knows us by name, our personality and individuality. It's a terrible thing to be unknown. We live in fear that we will never be known enough that others will never know who we really are, what our dreams are and where we are. We have nothing to fear because like those sheep in the ancient flock we are known by the Master Shepherd.

God knows you and me, everybody in his world who affirms His saviorship, His shepherdhood. The beauty and mystery about our Lord, our Shepherd is that if are lost or any one of His sheep is lost, He will look for us, hunt us, find us and bring as back to the fold.

It's true our lives are full of uncertainties, risk and danger. Today or tomorrow we don't know what's going to happen. The unexpected makes us fear. We cannot control tomorrow. We can only trust our Shepherd's wisdom and love to carry us through life's joys, pitfalls and the unknown. How will I know what to do today and tomorrow? I cannot tell you. All I know is that when the time comes to know, we know. Indeed, this is paradoxical. As George McDonald, a wise preacher, said: "Do not fear the how. The goodness is that the One who invites us on the journey accompanies and supplies our needs."

Verse 4: "Even when walking through the dark valley of death I will not be afraid, for you are close beside me, guarding, guiding all the way." (LB)

"Even if I go through the deepest darkness, I will not be afraid, Lord, for you are with me. Your shepherd's rod and staff protect me." (NRSV)

"And when I walk through the valley, overshadowed by death, I will fear no harm, for you are with me." (CP)

This is my favorite verse in the Shepherd Psalm. Note that the Lord is with us as we go through life, bright and dark, and into the life beyond, literally taking us by hand, shielding us from danger, and assuring us with His comfort in the face of darkness, in the way the shepherd of old, kept watch over his sheep. So should we be afraid and fear any danger as we walk through the valleys dark and dreadful? The Lord says: Never fear. I'll be with you always to the end of the world. It takes a quantum leap of faith to feel His Presence in our life.

He is here, there, and beyond, right beside us He is overwhelmingly alive, real, beyond our wildest dreams. The Shepherd who walks with us, who is within us, and around us, is the real presence. He is not a human construct, a theory or a projection of ourselves.

The evils that beset us, such as diseases, crime, disabilities, or hunger, were not willed by God but rather the results of the weaknesses of our human existence. God has provided the knowledge, know how, to scientists to find the cure of these evils so that man and woman will be made whole, if not in this world, in the next,

Indeed death casts the most frightening shadow for all of our lives, because we are the most helpless in its presence. We can struggle with many other enemies—pain, suffering, weaknesses, blindness and so forth, but cannot wrestle with death. That is one final enemy that God will conquer and vanquish. God has the final say on this matter. Only God can walk with us, no one else, through the death's abysmal darkness and safely bring us to the other side. With the time of our death uncertain, we should follow the Shepherd, our Lord and Master, with eternal confidence.

This eternal confidence was expressed by Todd Beamer on that hijacked Flight 93 as the plane hurtled towards destruction when he said to his fellow passengers: "Are you guys ready? Let's roll." This is paraphrasing in short order the David's words: "I walk through the valley of death, I will fear no evil." Todd Beamer could not have known that his words of confidence as he face imminent death was heard by millions. That the story of his last acts on earth would be a witness to the Lord he loved and served and a lasting example of heroism. Todd Beamer died as he lived, a faithful believer in the Good Shepherd.

Verse 5: "You provide delicious food for me in the presence of my enemies. You welcomed me as your guest, blessings overflow." (LB)
"You prepare a banquet for me, where all my enemies can see me; you welcome me as an honored guest and fill my cup to the brim." (GNB)

"Your rod and staff—they comfort me. You spread a table before me in face of my greatest fears. You drench my head with oil, my cup overflows the brim." (CP)

This verse expands on the idea of the Shepherd as a provider, protector and comforter. Note the mention of a table of food, a cup of wine and oil; staple provisions during the time of David. The elements symbolizes the Lord's great love and blessings.

Bishop Kenneth Carder of Nashville, Tenn. said that the Master Shepherd of David is the Jesus of today. He is the same. Jesus who commands "Come follow me" in this unending pilgrimage toward the kingdom of God. To quote the bishop; "Following the Master Shepherd is often dangerous, exhausting, and costly. The journey takes us through the wilderness of temptation, gardens of anguish, hillsides of crucifixion, and tombs of death and grief." But the Good Shepherd is there with us, helping us face valiantly these enemies to our existence. We must be confident that He will see us through with flying colors.

Verse 6: "Your goodness and unfailing kindness shall be with me all my life, and afterwards I will live with you forever in your home." (LB)

"I know that your goodness and love will be with me all my life; and your house will be my home as I live." (GNB)

"Surely goodness and kindness will accompany me all the days of my life and I will dwell in the house of the Holy for the length of my days." (CP)

What a resounding comfort that our Shepherd has assured us a place in His house. Note that as we journey through life His goodness, love and mercy shall follow us towards that place "not made with hands, but eternal in the heavens." David's word "surely" denotes a fact as certain as it is comforting. If we follow the Good Shepherd, our Lord he will surely bless us with goodness and love each day of our life on earth, and note, we shall live forever in the home of the Lord. He follows, shadowing us, attending us, assuring us that no matter what transpires today, or tomorrow, God will surround us with His goodness and love.

The concluding verses of Psalm 23 complete the final scenery which awaits us. Once more we are comforted and reassured with this unexpected simplicity "God is my Shepherd, there is nothing I lack." Every day, whether we know it or not, we're being led down the path that leads us home to the ultimate reality, our Father's home. This Shepherd, our Lord and Master, has taken us through the rugged terrain of life and now leads to the final place, where He has prepared a place for us to live forever. In this world or in the next, He is all we need.

I'd like to close with a prayer of David from Psalm 25: 4-5. (NRSV)

"Make us know your ways, Oh Lord. Teach me the paths. Guide me in your truth and teach me for you are the God of my salvation. I wait for you all day long." Amen.

7

OUR COVENANT WITH GOD

Deut. 6:4-9; 11:18-24

Good morning. My message today is based on the book of Deuteronomy. It is one of my favorite books in the Old Testament and the others are Exodus and Leviticus, because of their historical content. These historical books tell us of the Israelites and dynamic personalities who shaped the nation. And one of them is the historical Moses.

Moses was a towering figure in the Old Testament. He was the stuff of movie legends, such as the Ten Commandments. Deuteronomy contains the record of his speeches, injunctions, and ordinances. The Israelites were then newly freed from enslavement, and Moses provided the strong leadership and guidance during those difficult years of settling in the promised land.

Now who is Moses? The Biblical record shows that he is an early founder of ancient Israel, and its corresponding religion of Judaism. Abraham is considered the great leader by Christians, Jews and Muslims. Without him there would not be an Old Testament, no Jewish people, no Judaism and no Christian church. And perhaps no Islam, for Islam traces its origin to Moses, who is regarded as a prophet in their Holy Koran.

In Exodus, Leviticus, and Deuteronomy, we catch a vivid glimpse of his powerful personality. A leader of titanic proportions, inspired and equipped by God, to lead the Israelites out of the bondage in Egypt. He is described as a man with a hot, impetuous temper, a wise judge, slow of speech (perhaps a stutterer) a worker of miracles, a fighter, humble, selfless, and in modern day language, a workaholic, never resting, and never giving up.

He is still comes alive today as we read about him in Exodus and Deuteronomy, like he were striding across the pages of time and history, more than three millennia, leading thousands of half-nomads, across unchartered wilderness under the light of Jehovah.

Such a colossal character commands our attention and respect. For Moses is contemporary as a modern day statesman and religious personality for the lessons he is telling us as Christians.

On their trek to the Promised Land, the Israelites stopped by the land of Moab. Before they were to cross over the boundary, Moses recalls for the people the great events of the past forty years, and appeals to them to remember how God had led them through the wilderness and to be obedient and loyal to Jehovah. Moses reviews the Ten Commandments and emphasizes the meaning of the commandments, calling the people to give their devotion to the Lord alone, warning them against idolatry, and telling them the blessings of obedience to God of long and prosperous years ahead. And they will become a great nation.

Furthermore, Moses reminds the people of the meaning of God's covenant with them. He wants the people to renew their commitments to God. The God who led them as a pillar of cloud, showered them with manna in the desert wherever and is now on the brink of crossing to the Promised Land.

We Filipinos who have come over to the United States have much in common with the ancient Israelites. Like them, we left our homeland to seek a better future for us and our families in the USA. Cora and I made the decision to emigrate to the US in 1968 when we felt there was no future for our family in the Philippines. Inspite of the fact that both of us were gainfully employed, there was not much to show for our industry. We wanted a better future for our four growing girls, advanced education and job opportunities. And believing in the promise of the Lord that all things work for good to them that love the Lord, we set out to the promised land, the USA in 1968.

Five years ago that was in 1986, I was one of the editors commissioned by the General Commission on Archives and History to write the history of Asian Americans and United Methodism in the United States. I edited the "Churches Aflame" book. In my research on how the Filipino-American churches developed, I was appalled by the humiliating stories of servitude and degradation of Filipinos in the earlier years at the hands of white supremacists on the West Coast, because they were classified as Orientals. Orientals were a despised lot at that time. Thus, they were treated as Chinese or Japanese. Filipinos couldn't join white churches, and so some of the pioneering Filipinos had to form their own congregations, and worshipped in run-down buildings. Like the Blacks, they were not allowed to dine in public restaurants. And since Filipinos were Orientals, the early Filipino preachers were joined with the California Oriental Provisional Conference. Then the Methodist Episcopal Church thought the Filipinos were of Hispanic stock, and so the developing Filipino churches were attached to the Mexican Provisional Conference.

Like the ancient Israelites, Filipinos are sojourners and travelers in the US. Travelers have to come together. And like the Israelites, we gathered together representing many tribes—Ilocanos, Tagalogs, Visayans, and Hilagaynons. Now we give thanks to our mother church, the United Methodist Church for enabling us to worship in our own churches. We have arrived in the Promised Land after years of wandering in the desert.

Let's go back to the word "covenant" in our analogy of the Israelites and the Filipinos. This covenant was that if they would follow God's commandments and worship Him as their only God, that He would be faithful, merciful and just to them. That God would protect them from their enemies and make their nation great. However, the Jews often times failed to keep the covenant. Many of them were tempted to follow the gods of the Amorites, Canaanites, and Perizites. Inspite of their many violations and transgressions of the covenant, God showed them that He was "merciful and gracious, slow to anger, and abundant in loving kindness and truth." God was forgiving in their iniquities or sins. God kept His part of the covenant. The Israelites did not.

We Filipinos had a covenant, too, with God when we left our homeland and emigrated to the United States of America. We brought our distinct religious and cultural traditions. Unfortunately, many of us have forgotten our covenant with God when we came in contact with the affluence of this society. I have met many of our countrymen and women who became morbidly engrossed in the daily "pursuit of happiness," such as bigger homes, more cars, and other status symbols. There is nothing wrong in this pursuit. It is the obsession of the pursuit, the total attention to these material things that many have neglected the most essential part of their lives-that of worshipping God who brought them to this promised land. The neglect of the spiritual aspects of life has stunted their growth in the house of God. Indeed, many of our countrymen have mixed up their priorities of living the good life.

But all is not dim in the horizon. There is a silver lining for our Filipino brethren. In my observation as I travel across this broad land, I came across several people who are keeping the covenant. Since I was elected president of the National Association of Filipino-American United Methodists, I endeavored to restore our neglected covenant by proposing the congregational development of ethnic Filipino Methodist churches. Since 1987 the emphasis of my administration was the location of cities where the possibility of developing churches were pin pointed. Our research of possible places was headed by the Reverend Alexander Ramos, a brilliant Filipino-American minister of the Minnesota Conference, who also outlined the strategy for developing new congregations. Thus, with funding provided by the Board of Global Ministries, several small congregations were established in Texas, California, Illinois, West Virginia, New York, and Washington. Several young Filipino ministers came from the Philippines to help in the burgeoning ministries. I personally wrote the history of several of these successful churches which appeared in the "Churches Aflame" book. Amazingly, the Holy Spirit gathered our scattered brethren into the fold of these incipient United Methodist churches. The growth of our Filipino United Methodist churches continues to this day. As of my last count, there are presently 29 Filipino-American UMCs in the West Coast, in Texas, Chicago, Seattle and New York. Indeed we are keeping the covenant. Most of these churches are now well established and mission minded.

Our covenant is strengthened as we join in worship. We made a covenant with God through Jesus Christ when we accepted Him as our Lord and Savior, and that we will keep the faith through our prayers, our presence, our gifts and our service.

As a people, we may have been oppressed as we made our entry points in the United States of America, but we were never forsaken by God, who is faithful, just, and merciful.

We may be dispersed in this vast land of freedom and opportunity, but we have not lost our identity as a distinct ethnic cultural group in the United Methodist Church.

We gather together as sojourners and travelers to refresh ourselves and draw strength in our own worship of God.

We are keeping the covenant.

Let's pray.

Almighty God and Heavenly Father, forgive us for our preoccupation with the material things in life and help us focus our attention to the things that matter in our covenant of faith in our journey in our adopted land. Open our eyes and heart that gratitude for all your love has made possible in our lives may overflow and touch those around us, our neighbors in this community. Amen

8

COMBAT FISHING

Matt. 4: 12-22; Roman 8: 28

Good morning. As many of you know, most people come to Alaska to fish. I didn't know this interest until Cora and I came here in 1992 to visit on the invitation of a great lady named Bea Shepard. One day John Page, your former minister, took us in his skip in the channel and Wow! I caught a respectable size kind of fish. I didn't even know what kind of fish it was. John wrapped the fish nicely with words written on the wrapper "Caught with Pride." We took the fish to Iowa, and told our girls about the thrill of fishing in Juneau. One of our girls did some research and found that the fish was a 2-lb. pink salmon.

Well, since that first fish I discovered that fishing at DIPAC was much more productive, especially when the salmon are coming in to spawn. And that's where I describe the action as combat fishing. That is you fish shoulder to shoulder with fellow visiting fishermen. In combat fishing, one of the rules of engagement is to help your neighbor bring in his or her catch to the dock. When one hooks a fish your neighbors pull in their line to avoid entanglements, gets the net ready, and help pull the combative fish on the dock. Then you can cast your line again.

We never forget a fishing trip with Larry and Maureen Weeks in their beautiful boat when they took us to fish in the channel. And wow again, I landed my first silver salmon, a 10-lb pounder. That event was historically photographed and the photo is now hanging in our computer room, to remind me of one of the most exciting sporting events in my life.

DIPAC is my best fishing place and also my best fishing ministry. There I meet a number of my fellow Ilocanos, Tagalogs and Visayans. Some of them are so kind that seeing me as a neophyte fisherman sometimes share me their catch. I always bring home a salmon for dinner.

Today I want to share with you my exciting experience in combat fishing and its application to our lives as Christians.

From our text today you will note that Jesus was walking beside the Sea of Galilee and saw two Galileans, Simon called Peter and his brother Andrew. They were casting a net into the lake for they were commercial fishermen. They fished for a living.

Jesus hailed them, and challenged them with his words: "O come follow me, and I will make you fishers of men." In all of their days of fishing, the brothers have never heard someone called them to be fishers of men. What's this stranger up to? Is he a prophet or something to be calling us to fish for men? But, strangely enough the brothers immediately responded. As our story says, they left their nets and followed him.

With the two converts, Jesus saw two other brothers who were also fishing. Apparently, that day was not a good day for fishing for the brothers Zebedee, James and John, and their father were not having much luck. They were pulling empty nets. Again Jesus challenged them to join him to be fishers of men. James and John left their father and joined Jesus in their quest for people.

Focus on the verse: "Come follow me and I will make you fishers of men."

That invitation to come and follow him is an invitation as well as a commandment. Let's go fish for people. Jesus uses the analogy of fishing as a method for spreading words of life and salvation. This is evangelization as we know it today.

In those ancient days, commercial fisher men used nets to catch fish. And by using the net you catch fish of all kinds, big or small, good and trash fish. There were no exceptions in the catch. When they dragged the net they caught all kinds of anything that swims in the sea of Galilee. Fish at that time were abundant. So commercial fisher men were catching tons of fish to feed the people who live along the shore, and perhaps sell the catch in the inland towns. Fish was the staple food of the Palestinians. Jesus used fish to feed thousands of people who assembled on the shore to hear him preach.

Incidentally, a friend of mine who was on a pilgrimage to the Holy Land told me that even today, the Sea of Galilee still has fish, which is called Peter's fish. However, he didn't see commercial fishing and men of the type of Simon Peter and Andrew. The Sea of Galilee remains as a tranquil body of water and historically significant since its connection to Jesus ministry.

My interest in fishing was kindled by a retired repairman of washing machines when I was doing graduate work at Syracuse University. His name was Al Gibson. He took me one time fishing at a nearby lake on his boat, and when in my first cast I caught a fish which turned out to be a two-pound big mouth bass, I was hooked to fishing for the rest of my graduate student days. I didn't catch fish every time we fish. We were skunked several times. And the joke about fishing is that "you should have been here yesterday." Although there are fish somewhere there in the bottom, they are not biting no matter what kind of bait or lure you are using. I wonder why?

Have you ever watched one of those sports fishing shows? Watching those fisherman hooked and release pull lunkers. They made me envious of their luck. I began to see later that those shows were edited to make it appear that they are always successful. They don't show the real side fishing. You cast many times before you can even get a single hit. From my experience at DIPAC, I'd say that out of 20 casts I get a bite or a hit; Other fishers get a bite on their first cast. So fishermen are not created equal on the fishing dock. Some are lucky, others are just not too lucky.

Now what about those disciples who were recruited by Jesus to be fishers of men. Why did Jesus choose them to do a job which was entirely different from their usual occupation? Were they any good?

In answer to those questions, may I hazard a guess. Jesus chose them because He knew by their looks, strong healthy persons, open minds and enterprising dispositions they want to venture to another calling. While fishing may have been lucrative for them, they sensed that the call of Jesus to be fishers of men sounded more challenging and meaningful. Fishers of men for the kingdom of God. That's the essence of Jesus' call to these early disciples. To these disciples, Jesus sent them out into the mass of humanity in early Palestine to share the good news of salvation. They didn't chose their audience. They preached to all kinds of people-poor, rich, downtrodden, sick, infirmed, and prisoners. They cast their message in an ocean of people. They netted some, and perhaps discarded the incorrigibles. These venture of evangelization was perhaps the most exciting aspect of their discipleship. Jesus was with them all the way.

Consider then that we are the modern day representatives of Jesus' ancient disciples. We who are called to do the fishing in our communities that is filled with people of all kinds—rich, poor, sick, hungry, lonely, and so forth. Often times, we say that to go out and carry on the message of love and charity to these people is the job of the minister, the trained pastor, and professional care givers. Some times we join these care givers for compliment, that is to perform a perfunctory duty, not with a heart full of compassion. We avoid the nitty-gritty part of our witness, and chose the easy part without sweat. That is we are not involved in combat evangelism.

Since we came to Juneau, Cora and I have met many of our countrymen and women in all walks of life—on their job sites, on the street, in their homes, at fishing docks, parties, weddings, baptisms, and so forth. We begun to see them in action and reaction to our witness. Some react positively, others indifferent, and a few negatively. We have cast our message in the sea of people. We have cast our nets many times in formal and informal conversation about our mission in the community. To us it didn't matter whether we were catching the trophy fish or any kind of fish. Many times like in real fishing, some of our catches manage to get away. They broke our line. As with lunkers, you have to have a steel leader to hold them. Still we followed our strategy of personal evangelism—call, visit and invite.

Casting our message is all that counts in our fishing for men. We have casts so many times. Sometimes, there were hits or bites, many times there were none. Zero, nil.

But we kept on casting. This is where fishing in the lake and fishing in the community have something in common. And that is patience and endurance. People we are reaching are not going to come and jump into our net or hit our lure. To share our message, our witness in an uncertain pool of fish is a challenging endeavor. I admire the patience and compassion of other fellow fishers of men like the Jehovah's Witnesses who knocked on doors with their pamphlets and announcements of evangelistic rallies. They are all working like us for the Kingdom of God.

I had an experience once while on an Alaskan airline winging its way to Juneau. Sitting beside me was a Filipino who was on his way to Kenai to work in a cannery. In the course of our conversation, and incidentally he was a fellow Ilocano, my language which we carried on in our exchange of views, I discovered that he had not read the Bible or gone to church—being a Roman Catholic. I told him that if he wished I could arrange to send him a Bible, and mark some of my favorite verses for him to read. His response was positive. I sent him the Bible and underline my favorite verse: John 3:16. A favorite verse to me because that was the first verse I learned from our Sunday School teacher in the Philippines. I cast my fishing pole and got a bite. It was not a King Salmon, but a real fish, a real person. I thanked God that I was there at the right time and place when I cast my pole.

Now to go back to my analogy of fishing, Jesus calls us to be fishers. This means we are not alone in the process of proclaiming the Good News. God is with us, since it is God the Holy Spirit who enables us to cast our message that it will reach the heart and mind of our people. It is the Holy Spirit who does the catching. We don't take the rejection of our message personally. We have done our job of casting.

Jesus sends us out to fish in the waters of humanity— in all kinds of weather—stormy, rainy, snowy, windy and peaceful. In our experience, we have visited with families in this community facing all kinds of problems and issues—illnesses, divorces, drug problems, overwork, death, and so forth. These are some of the situations which we have been confronted. Sometimes we don't cast our message of hope and salvation. We comfort them with our prayers and compassionate listening.

Our Savior went fishing for us and caught us by His grace. Jesus considered you and me as "Keepers." He did not want to throw us back like trash fish into the murky waters of sin and unbelief. He reached us and kept us with his love and mercy. Jesus did not use a cane pole or a graphite rod with Zebco reel, or even a net. Jesus use rugged plank of wood and some rusty nail for his attraction. He used himself as the bait or lure. He allowed himself to be hung on the cross for the entire world to see, so that all might witness the power of his love and sacrifice.

Someone took the time to share that powerful message with you. The Holy Spirit worked in your heart and mine, creating faith in Jesus our Savior, and we were caught! It has a little to do with you or me, and it has everything to do with the amazing grace of our Savior-God.

We don't rely on ourselves to share the Good News. And we don't rely on other people to be ready to receive it. Think about it. How many people like fish really want to be caught? It's the same thing with people. By nature, we ourselves when left alone too long are sinful and hostile. We are afraid of Him. There's nothing we can do to condition ourselves to be ready to be caught. We cannot take any credit for our faith in Jesus Christ any more than we can take credit for leading some to faith.

It has little to do how good we are, and it has everything to do with the grace of our Savior.

The early disciples—Peter, Andrew, James and John, were not the greatest fishers of men. They didn't have a formal education. Time and again, they proved how spiritually ignorant they were. Think of Peter. He was so impetuous, quick to anger, like they say, had a short fuse. He was the one, who on the night of Jesus' betrayal, insisted that he would rather go to the cross with Jesus rather than deny Him. And just a couple of hours later, we find Peter crying in the dark because a young woman challenged his faith. And this is the one Jesus called the Rock. James and John were also described as arrogant and foolish. They foolishly thought they could sit at Jesus' right and left in power and authority when He fulfilled his ministry. They had no idea of what kind of kingdom Christ was establishing. These men had a lot of misgivings concerning Christ. Yet Jesus was gracious; he sought them out to be fishers of men. He has done the same with us.

How true that is with many of us who were caught by our Savior. In the process of practicing our faith, we are cleansed by the "blood of the Lamb," our Savior who died on the cross to take away our sins and made acceptable as the redeemed. The Holy Spirit has caught us with the Gospel—leading us to believe in Jesus Christ, the son of God and the Son of Man. He has saved us in the waters of baptism, showering us with His redemption.

The Holy Spirit has placed the perfect fishing equipment in our hands. It's not a tackle box full of baits or lures. It's the sweet message of sins forgiven in Jesus' name. Above all, we have God's promise to bless our efforts as He sees fit. All we need is to do is spread our nets and share the Gospel of Jesus Christ. God will do the rest.

Let's pray.

Almighty and Gracious God, you called the four fishermen to leave their nets and follow you. Help us today to be open to your leading as we seek ways to follow You and share the Good News of your love with all the people You enable us to meet. In Jesus 'name and for His sake we pray. Amen.

9

IS THERE ANY HOPE?

Matt. 28:1-10; 1 Peter 1: 1-9

Good Morning. In the middle of Word War 2, an American submarine was badly foundering off the coast of California. Severely damaged from a fight with Japanese destroyers, the sub managed to ride out the rough seas in an attempt to make it back to port in San Diego. While still almost a day from safe harbor, the icy sea managed to choke out the engine. The sub slowly sank to the bottom of the ocean carrying all aboard with it.

A full two days later an American destroyer arrived on the scene and sent frogmen down to the sub. They used their grappling hooks and knives to bang on the sides of the submarine in an attempt to see if there were any survivors. Then, through the stillness, they waited. From the inside of the disabled craft, came a message in Morse code:

Is there any hope?

Every day we are bombarded with bad news-wars, floods, murder, kidnapping, and so forth. On top of all these, we are faced with personal problems like depression, bitterness, sorrow, and so forth. So amidst all these world-wide and personal problems, we are confronted with the age-old question, Is there any hope for me, for you and for the people of the world? How do we deal with these situations?

Now before I answer the question, you must know that it is not really my answer. The answer comes from God; for I'm just a messenger of what God in Christ has sent me to do today. In preparing this message I have gone over our Bible, and consulted the writings of great men, like John Wesley and contemporary religious leaders. And they all say we should not despair; we should not be beaten down by all the bad news in this world, whether it is happening to us, or our family, or the community in general, because beyond all of these things there is a living hope, there is a bright light at the end of the tunnel. That is good news to me, and I tell you why.

Our scripture says, in the words of Peter:

"All honor to God, the God and Father of our Lord Jesus Christ; for it is his boundless mercy that has given us the privilege of being born again, so that we are now members of God's own family. Now we live in the hope of eternal life because Christ rose again from the dead.

And God has reserved for his children the priceless gift of eternal life; it is kept in heaven for you, pure and undefiled, beyond the reach of change and decay. And God in his mighty power, will make sure that you get there safely to receive it, because you are trusting him. It will be yours in that coming last day for all to see. So be truly glad! There is wonderful joy ahead, even though the going is rough for a while down here" (1 Peter 1:3-6 LB)

Are we really hopeless in the midst of all these troubles? Of course not! In fact the last sentence in the Living Bible, "There is wonderful joy ahead, even though the going is rough for a while down here."

But how can we have joy in the midst of a rough world? How can you comfort someone whose son was killed in Iraq? A friend whose children were murdered by a senseless killer? Someone who can't find a job? Someone who has been deserted by a father?

We do not understand how all these evil things are happening in this world, and to some of us, who have experienced problems of huge proportions, or perhaps even now some of you are facing enormous troubles. And like Job we ask, where is God? Why is this happening to me, my friend, my family? God's ways are unknowable? Unfathomable. There are many things in this world that are beyond our grasp and understanding. Science can explain what causes diseases, illnesses, and many health problems. But doctors cannot tell you why these diseases are in this world. Why do tsunamis happen? Shifting of tectonic plates, but still why?

Even though we find no answer to our problems at present, there is one thing I want you to know. We know there is hope. And we seriously need hope, a living hope. We need a living hope on which we can anchor our lives to be able to survive in our world today.

A number of years ago researchers performed an experiment to see the effect of hope on living with hardships. Two sets of laboratory rats were placed in tubs of water. The researchers left one set in the water and found that within in an hour they had all drowned. The other set of rats were periodically lifted out of the water and then returned. When that happened, the second set of rats swam for 24 hours. Why? Not because they were given rest, but because they suddenly had hope. Those animals somehow hoped that if they could stay afloat just about a little longer, someone could reach down and rescue them.

We need hope. It is as simple as that. But what kind of hope? There is hope that is just that—a hope. A hope like—I hope it doesn't rain tomorrow. Or I hope I go to heaven when I die. Some have hope in their jobs. Others have hope in their doctor. Have you seen that old man putting coins in the slot machine hoping to win that million dollars?

In the Philippines, the sweepstakes is widely popular source of hope for people. They hope that someday they'll win the million peso prize. Such hopes are wishful thinking. Its an unfounded desire for things to go as we wish. The help of such hope is minimal at best, or misleading or damaging at most.

"Our living hope is founded on the promises of God. Our Hope as Christians is rooted in the God and Father of Jesus Christ. And He can never fail. His word is true. His promises are sure. His salvation is eternal."

There is no other source of eternal hope. God says, "Do not be afraid. I am with you. I will gather you from east and west, from south and north." Many world religions and philosophies, like Buddhism, Hinduism, or even Islam offer some kind of hope for the world and the next, but all are inadequate. Even the most promising philosophy of this world will seem rather empty when a person is about to cross over to the other side, eternity. (Isaiah 43: 5)

Tell me where in the Bible does it say: "God helps those who help themselves." Actually, that does not come from the Bible. It is just a common saying. The Bible says just the contrary. God helps those who are helpless and hopeless. God helps those who are sunk, are beaten down. Those who have had it. That is the kind of a person the Lord reaches out for.

Our hope as Christian is built on nothing else than Christ. 1 Cor. 13 tells us that one of the greatest gifts God gives us is hope. But how can we gain hope?

Roman 15: 4 says we gain hope by "endurance of steadfastness." The Bible teaches: "For whatever was written in former days was written for our instructions, so that by steadfastness and by encouragement of the scriptures we might have hope."

It is God's good pleasure to give the desire of your heart. But, its God's practice not always to give us what we want when we want it. Thus, we learn to wait upon God and learn endurance.

So to attain God's kind of hope is by steadfastness or endurance. We walk among people who are without hope. Let's get busy sowing seeds of hope in this hopeless world around us.

It is our responsibility to sow the seeds of hope in others. 1 Peter 3:18 urges: "Always be ready to make your defense to anyone who demands from you an accounting for the hope that is in you."

The Word of God fills us with hope, because it gives us examples of the faithfulness of God and the way in which He can and will work in our lives. God cannot lie and will always keep his promises.

In Hebrews 6:13 states: "When God made a promise to Abraham, because he had no one greater by whom to swear, he swore by himself, saying "'I will surely bless you and multiply you.'"

"We have this hope, a sure and steadfast anchor of the soul, a hope that enters the inner shrine behind the curtain, where Jesus, a forerunner in our behalf, has entered, having become a high priest forever according to the order of Melchizedeck." (Hebrews 6: 19-20)

Lastly, our hope is in a Person. And that is Jesus Christ. It is hope that is centered in the Person of Christ our savior.

1 Peter 1:6-9 says: In this you rejoice even if now for a little while you have to suffer serious trials, so that the genuiness of your faith—being more precious than gold that, though perishable, is tested by fire—may be found to result in praise and glory and honor when Jesus is revealed. Although you have not seen him, you love him; and even though you do not see him now, you believe in him and rejoice with an indescribable and glorious joy, for you are receiving the outcome of your faith, the salvation of your soul."

In these verses Peter is telling us that though we have not seen Jesus in Person with our physical eyes we must have to see Jesus our Savior with the eye of faith. That is the key to our hope in Christ—our eye of faith. This eye transcends beyond the physical world. Our intellect as human beings does not enable us to grasp the reality of Jesus Christ. Only our faith in Him gives us the grasp of what we cannot see or feel with our human senses.

Do you remember the famous editorial in the *New York Sun* entitled "Yes Virginia, there is a Santa Claus." This editorial was an answer to an 8-year old girl name Virginia O'hanlon, who wrote a letter to the editor asking for a confirmation as to whether or not there is a Santa Claus, since her father was not sure about Santa Claus.

I love this editorial, and you know what? Since it was published in 1897, it has been printed every year during Christmas time by countless newspapers and magazines.

I like the last paragraph of Frank Church's editorial, which I am quoting as follows:

"You tear the baby's rattle and see what makes the noise inside. but there is a veil covering the unseen world which not the strongest man, nor even the united strength of all the strongest men that ever lived could tear apart. Only faith, poetry. love, romance can push aside that curtain and view and picture the supernal beauty and story beyond. Is it real? Ah, Virginia, in all this world there is nothing else real and abiding."

Now, we see the reality of Jesus Christ only through the eyes of faith. And if so, then our hopes for the future, our hopes for a better world, our hopes for the answers to our prayers are confirmed and assured. Our hope for our salvation is assured by our faith in Him.

It is this hope in Jesus Christ that keeps us going everyday in the midst of our disappointments, trials, difficulties and illnesses.

As Peter affirms, the true Christian should be the most joyous person that walks the earth. This joy should show through our eyes, through our faces, through our expression. through our body language, through everything about you. Everything about you should speak to others about our living hope in Christ Jesus who has saved you and me, through his death, burial and resurrection. That's why the Christian faith is the most joyous in the world. Christians are the most joyous people in the world, because they have a living hope. When we talk about witnessing for our faith, do the words of our mouth match the reality of our living hope in Christ?

There is a story about Joseph Scriven who gave most of his life and energy to those who could not repay him. In his youth, he had the prospect of being a great citizen with high ideals and great aspirations. He was engaged to a beautiful woman who had promised to share his dream, but on the eve of their wedding her body was pulled from a pond into which she had accidentally fallen and drowned. Young Scriven never overcame the shock. Although a college graduate and ready to embark on a brilliant career, he began to travel to try to forget his sorrow. His wanderings took him to Canada where he spent the last forty-one of his sixty years. He became a very devout Christian. His beliefs led him to do manual labor for poor widows and sick people. He often served for no wages. A friend who was living with discovered a poem Scriven had written to his mother in a time of sorrow. His poem was later set to music and has become a much love Gospel song. What was this poem?

> *"What a friend we have in Jesus,*
> *All our sins and griefs to bear.*
> *What a privilege to carry,*
> *Everything to God in prayer.*
> *Oh, what peace we often forfeit,*
> *Oh, what needless pain we bear;*
> *All because we do not carry,*
> *Everything to God in prayer."*

Is there any hope in a world of hopelessness?

God through the gospel of our Lord Jesus Christ, has answered a resounding Yes!

There is hope because our sins have been paid for upon the cross of Calvary. There is hope because the Body of Christ was placed in a tomb. There is hope because on the third day Jesus rose from the dead. There is hope because the Devil couldn't deceive him. Death couldn't stop him, and the grave couldn't hold Him.

There is living hope because of the Resurrection and that is the key to our Christian faith. This is the living hope which we all look forward to. Why? Just as He said: Jesus rose from the dead. We can be confident, therefore, that he will accomplish all He has promised. It is the living and abiding Word of God that is our living hope.

What did you bring with you this morning? Fear? Wrong motives? Anxiety of what tomorrow may bring? Despair over physical problems?

My friends, is the Lord your portion this morning? Is He your everything? If He is, you can have living hope for the future. Don't give up. Listen to Jeremiah: "The Lord is my portion. Therefore I have hope in Him."

I close with this verse from Romans 15: 13:

"May the God of hope fill you with all the joy and peace as you trust in him, so that you may overflow with hope by the power of the Holy Spirit," Amen.

10
SHAPED FOR SERVING GOD

❧❧

1 Peter 4: 10-11

Good morning. I wonder if many of you have read or heard about the horrendous crime story of Ashley Smith from Duluth, Georgia, last month when she was held hostage by Brian Nichols for seven frightening hours in her apartment. Brian had allegedly overpowered a guard and murdered a judge, a court stenographer, a federal agent, and sheriff's deputy, and seriously injured a police woman and newspaper reporter.

He fled on a stolen pickup truck and ended in front of the apartment of Ashley Smith about 2 a.m. Saturday. At that time Ashley went to a convenience store for some cigarettes and on her return noticed a man in a truck in the parking lot. As she started to put the key in the door of her apartment, Brian was right there behind and jabbing a gun on her side. She let out a blood curdling scream.

"Don't scream," he warned her. "If you don't scream, I won't hurt you." Then he forced her into the bathroom.

Now here's the terrifying side of her ordeal. After Brian Nichols hogtied her, Ashley opened up a conversation with him inspite of the fact that she was trembling with fear while her own life was on the line. She bravely asked him if she could read a page of the book *Purpose Driven Life,* a Christian inspirational bestseller which her aunt had given her earlier. Brian said yes. That is after he had a shower and indicated a glimmer of hope in his blood red eyes.

This is the last sentence "We serve God by serving others." And she continued reading two more paragraphs. The words struck a sympathetic chord in the heart of Brian who asked her what she thought he should do. She bravely gave it straight to him, "I think you should turn yourself in, lots more people are going to get hurt, and you're probably going to die."

Wow! Brave words spoken by a woman whose life was at the mercy of a killer. He easily would have snuffed out her life like those four persons he had just killed two days ago. Ashley Smith was no stranger to violence. She almost lost her life four years ago when she and her husband were involved in a Friday bar free-for-all. Her husband was fatally stabbed, and eventually died in her arms.

Earlier her life was a mess as she was into drugs and petty crimes. At that time when Brian Nichols showed up she was just beginning to turn her life around by moving to Duluth where she found a waitressing job while she was enrolled in a medical assistant program at a community college.

Did Ashley Smith's reading of a part of the book *Purpose Driven Life* help catch an alleged killer? My answer to the question would be: "Of course, it did."

Yes, indeed Smith's faith, patience, and determination saved her own life as well as Brian Nichols who was eventually arrested.

For helping in the arrest of an alleged criminal Ashley Smith was hailed as a hero by the press. Smith is my type of hero. Her refusal to panic in the face of terrifying circumstances qualified her being heroic. She had grace under pressure, coolness under fire!

Now let me go back to that statement: "*We serve God by serving others.*" We can draw our first lesson from Ashley Smith's experience. Indeed she exemplified greatness of self. She served God by leading a violent man to the path of righteousness.

God is testing us by asking us to serve in ways where we're not familiar. Ashley Smith was not trained to talk to a criminal, much less to lead him to a non-violent ending. And yet like we say she rose to the occasion. Met naked danger in the face, and turned around what could have been a disastrous outcome.

It is not very often that we face perilous situations as Ashley Smith's wherein we are called to serve in dangerous situations. But there are plenty of circumstances where we are challenged to do so. For example: here's Rick Warren's simple illustration in his book "If you see a drunk fall by the street, God expects you to help him, and not to say 'I'm not a policeman or a social worker. I don't want to be involved. He is not my problem. I've got some other important business to attend to."

Well, its true. You may not be any of these people, but your help is urgently needed at that moment. You reveal yourself at the moment. No special talent is needed to lend a helping hand to that poor drunk lying helplessly by the wayside, who might be in danger of losing his life. Your helping hand reveals your character.

It is the common, humdrum situations, in our daily lives that we are confronted with fellow human beings who are in need of your helping hand, words of comfort, and whole hearted assistance.

As you all know, Douglas Community United Methodist Church has been the beneficiary of many Volunteer in Mission teams, that include a VIM team from our church in Cedar Falls, Iowa. And even now these teams are busy at work serving Douglas church doing painting, carpentering, renovating, gardening, counselors, teachers and so forth. In 1997 our Iowa VIM did some heavy duty excavation work around the parsonage to water proof the basement. VIM teams are serving God with their hands, talents and gifts. They came here on their own time and resources, not to glorify themselves, but for the glory of God, to serve others, to see that this church will become a beacon on the hill.

Are you available to serve God anytime? We may not be shaped to do heroic deeds, but we are called to do the simple, mundane chores which will improve the lives of helpless impoverished persons. As a servant of God, you don't get to pick and choose when or where you will serve.

At this point I must confess to you that I had what you call my "druthers." That is, I had earlier doubted about our possible return to Alaska to continue our Filipino-American ministry. After my thyroid surgery last year I told Cora that perhaps we may not be able to return because of my needed recuperation. Also, I was ready to retire, and we laid our plans to retire in Fairfield, Iowa, to join our daughter and her family. Yet, by the grace of God, and strengthened by prayers I was able to regain my health to stand before you today to deliver God's message.

God called us through the little voice of a great woman in this church, Bea Shepard, to come back and serve again to a service that we love and enjoy. Nobody retires when God calls to serve in His name.

Our key verse says: "God has given each of you special abilities, be sure to use them to help each other, passing on to others God's many kinds of blessings. Are you called to preach as though God himself were speaking through you. Are you called to help others? Do it with all the strength and energy that God supplies, so that God will be glorified through Jesus Christ—to him be the glory and power forever and ever."

Note the key words in the verse that each of us is given—"special abilities" to serve. Special abilities does not mean we have to be an expert of something, or a professional, to be shaped to serve. To work on even the most menial task does not require special abilities.

The bottom line is this: It does not require special talent to stay after a meeting to pick up trash or stack chairs after a meeting. It does not require special talent to serve at the Glory Hole, volunteer in the annual barbecue, and so forth. Anyone is shaped up to be a servant of God. All it requires is character. Serving like Jesus Christ means making ourselves available, if we are able.

Proverbs 3: 27-28 urges "Do not withhold good to those with whom it is due, when it is in your power to do it. Do not say to your neighbor "Go, and come again tomorrow I will give it, when you have it with you."

And now I come to my second point

That is real servants of God do their best with what they have.

The Body of Christ, which is the church, will grow if we all heed this point. We are all disciples. You and I are part of the Body of Christ. The body withers if it does not have the proper nourishment.

We should provide the nourishment by our discipleship—our witness so the Body of Christ grows to its full potential. As servants of Christ we should do our best with what we have, our time, talent, gifts and presence in every opportunity. If you wait for the perfect conditions you will never get anything done. Disciples of Christ don't make excuses, procrastinate or wait for better times. One reason many people fail to serve is that they fear they are not good enough. They believe the lie that only superstars are called to do the job. God has made us for a purpose. To do His will and glorify Him.

Rick Warren's success as a church leader and eventual huge success of his Saddleback Church in California is based on the "good principle." That is God does not have to have perfect people to do the job for Him. Warren says: "He would rather involve hundreds of regular folks in the ministry of the church than have a perfect church run by a few elites."

Douglas church has a lot of people who have made and continue to make a difference in this community. And I challenge my felllow Filipino-Americans who are here now to serve the church; to make your witness count by your involvement in church programs, activities, and worship services to name a few, in which the church ministry is called upon where Christ is lifted up. This community has many of our countrymen and women whom we call "unchurched," who seldom go to church or not at all, forgetting their roots and spending more time in making a living. That's why Cora and I continue to enjoy our Ministry of the Presence—which we call, visit and invite our Filipino compatriots in this community.

The Bible says "If you think you are too important to help someone in need, you are only fooling yourself. You are really a nobody." (Galatians 6:3)

One last point: *As real servants of Jesus Christ we must be faithful to our ministry.*

We are all involved in the ministry of Jesus Christ— serving people by our gifts, resources, talents, and presence or availability.

In other words we have to be faithful to our responsibilities in our job and chosen careers. We must fulfill our promises and complete our commitments, like if we volunteered to be a committee member tasked to do something, then do the job. We don't leave a job half done, and we don't quit when we get discouraged. Real servants of Christ are trustworthy and dependable.

Imagine what it will feel like one day to have God say to you:

"Well done, my good and faithful servant. You have been faithful in handling this small amount, so now I will give you many more responsibilities. Let's celebrate."

Let's pray the Prayer of Ignatious Loyola

"Teach us, good Lord,
To serve you as you deserve;
To give and not count the cost;
To fight and not heed the wounds;
To toil and not to seek for rest;
To labor and not to ask for any reward;
Except that of knowing that we do your will;
Through Jesus Christ our Lord."

Amen

11

HOW GOD WANTS OUR CHURCH TO GROW

Acts 2:42-47; James 2:24-26

Good morning. I would like to share with you my thoughts on how God wants our church to grow abundantly.

Our home church in Cedar Falls, Iowa, has this statement of purpose printed on the church bulletin each Sunday. It says "Our purpose is to glorify God by making disciples for Christ." Below the statement are two words—Pastors—names of the two pastors, and Ministers—the entire congregation.

So we lay people are all ministers. What do we mean by the word minister? That's what I want to explore with you today. We take this word for granted sometimes, and it has never been fully explained to me its meaning and implication. So I did some research.

In the polity or organization of the United Methodist Church, the pastors are called and addressed as reverends. They are academically and theologically trained people and are graduates of seminaries, also called schools of theology. The UMC has hundreds of seminaries in the world. Graduates apply for assignment to a state conference and a period of apprenticeship serving full time in a local church and if their performance is acceptable, meeting rigorous requirements, they are then recommended for ordination as elders. They are appointed by the bishop to a church congregation. As long as they perform well they are usually appointed to a pastoral charge on a yearly basis.

Now what about us—members of the church—the lay people, we are called ministers. We are not trained like the pastors. How can we be ministers? Since I was born, bred and baptized in the Methodist church, I never found the distinction of a pastor and minister. In the Philippines, a person who is in charge of the church is the pastor and minister. My late dad who was a Methodist minister for fifty years was always addressed as "Pastor." In this sense the pastor is like the shepherd—the leader of the flock. The American missionaries has always called the Filipinos as pastors of the church. In the United States, the ministers are the members of the whole congregation.

We are indeed ministers, people who listen to the Word of God each Sunday. The early disciples were ministers. None of them went through seminary. Except for Paul who had training under Rabbi Gamaliel, the rest of the apostles were ministers. They received their training from Jesus Christ, who instructed them to go and "make disciples in all nations, baptizing them into the Father, and the Son, and of the Holy Spirit" and teach these new disciples to obey all the commands I have given you, and be sure of this—that I am with you always to the end of the world." And by their ministry the Christian church spread throughout the ancient world. Their ministry was that they were witnesses of what Jesus Christ did for the people. That through His death and resurrection people would have eternal life.

The instructions and commandments of Jesus Christ still apply to us today as they did for those ancient disciples and those who followed the Christian faith. We lay people are the life of the church. Were we not here, and this applies to all other churches, there would be no congregation called the church, the Body of Christ. Thus, as members of the Body of Christ we have to grow, for a body that does not grow is either stunted, deformed, or dead.

Someone has said that between an airplane and every other form of locomotion and transportation there is one great contrast. The horse and wagon, the automobile, the locomotive, the speed boat, and the mighty battleship—all can come to a standstill without danger, and they can all reverse their engines, or their power, and go back.

But there is no reverse about the engine of an airplane, except its reverse thrust in jets when it slows the craft on landing. It cannot back up. It dare not standstill. If it loses its momentum and forward drive, then it crashes. The only safety for the airplane is in its forward and upward motion.

So the only safe direction for the Christian and for the church is forward and upward. If we Christians and ministers stop making forward progress, we are in danger of perishing in oblivion. We don't want that to happen. So the first thing that God requires of us is that He wants our church to grow deeper. Like a plant as it matures, its roots go deeper into the ground to reach the rich nutrients which sustains its growth.

Our verse instructs: "They joined with other believers in regular attendance of the apostles' teaching sessions and at the communion service and prayer meetings." (Acts 2: 42 LB).

We grow deeper in our faith being involved in the life of the church. Like the first Christians we must be in regular attendance in our worship service and teaching programs of our church, for example, Sunday Schools, Bible studies, and special classes conducted by our pastors and lay people trained in religious programs. We lay people in the United Methodist Church have a special program called "lay speaker's training" which trains us to make presentations of our witness. We are not pastors, but simply assistants to the pastors in one of his or her many duties and responsibilities, Being the pastor of a church is a huge responsibility—preaching, baptizing, officiating communions, weddings, and vital rituals and liturgies of the church, which we lay people are not trained to do. Therefore, it is our responsibility to do those things that the pastor can't always attend to.

1 Peter 2:2 urges: "Like new born infants, long for the pure, spiritual milk, so that by it you may grow into salvation. if indeed you tasted that the Lord is good."

As members of the Body of Christ, we need to grow in our involvement in the study of the scripture, the spiritual milk. Since our coming to Douglas Church Cora and I have always derived nourishment in the Bible study by Bea Shepard, whose insights borne of many years of experience in church work, have widened our understanding of the Christian faith and life.

At our church in Cedar Falls we are also regular attendees of a Bible class which is called Open Doors. Most coming are people of our age level, and in our lively discussions and sharing of perspectives we derive a deeper vision of our Christian faith. Did we grow spiritually as we are engaged in this kind of activity? Of course, we did. There is always something—new ideas, insights, point of views that are shared and those linger in our minds.

2 Peter 3:18 says: "But grow in the grace and knowledge of our Lord and Savior Jesus Christ." That is the whole key to growing in our Christian life, knowing more of the ways to follow Jesus Christ.

God wants our church to grow outward and upward. As ministers of the church it is our responsibility to see that we do our part of extending our witness beyond the building to our community. What are we witnessing for? The Bible reveals that we are witnessing for the "abundant life in Christ" that we members and ministers have experienced as we grow together in Christ's love and grace.

Then the second point is this: That for our church to grow we should grow together. Our key verse says: "And all believers met together constantly and shared everything with each other." (Acts 2:44 LB)

Besides growing deeper in our faith, we have to grow together. We have heard the common saying: "No man is an island." An island is an isolated piece of land usually in the middle of an ocean, lakes or rivers. It never grows. But, take a tree like what we see here in the forests of Alaska. They grow together luxuriantly, huge pine and spruce trees, which have weathered all kinds of weather for many years.

With this analogy, we too should grow together when we are with our fellow believers, members of the congregation. That is working together in activities—be it in corporate worship, church programs and fund campaigns which are all designed for the glory of God. We learn more of our faith by our actions. There is joy in being together like a big family, all involved in a task, activity, programs all which glorify God. We grow together in our faith as we study the scriptures and develop our prayer life. It is our togetherness that we remain strong and alive for and in Christ.

We gather—together in order to be that "redeemed and redeeming fellowship in which the Word of God is preached." We gather to understand more fully the nature of the call to witness and serve. It is not sufficient to hear and receive; one must share his or her faith in Christ Jesus.

In some religions, like the Hindu and the Buddhist, there are people called Holy Men. They meditate by themselves and are isolated from other believers in temples or remote places. We as Christians do not operate that way. There maybe times for privacy.

Overall, the Christian religion is a social oriented organization. It is a religion of fellowship. We interact with each other. We are all bound together by our belief in the saving grace of our Lord Jesus Christ. We share our faith together, and like the ancient Christians we share our faith with love by giving to meet certain missional needs of our community and world.

You were made for a mission. The word mission means "sending." Being a Christian includes being sent into the world, our community as a representative of Christ. Jesus said: "As the Father has sent me, I am sending you."

God wants you to have both a ministry in the Body of Christ and a mission in the world. Your ministry is your service to believers, and your mission is your service to unbelievers. In our ministry we must reach out to people in love. That is what will grow a church better than anything else.

A certain soap maker having run out of superlatives to define the perfection of his product, hit upon a statement which said in a novel and compelling way the last word that could be uttered concerning it: "As we couldn't improve our product, we improved the box."

So brothers and sisters, we can't improve on our product, because our product is the Lord Jesus. But, we can improve the box. That's us. We must improve us if the church is to grow.

The Bible says faith without action is dead. I would not be standing here today were it not for the early American missionaries who came to the Philippines in the early 1900s, preached their evangelical message, converted many people, like my late father and mother, and thus the evangelical faith spread like wild fire in the virgin lands of the Philippines. My wife and I are one of the offsprings of these "wild fires of the Holy Spirit."

Today, there are half a million Protestants in the Philippines. Thanks a million to the American missionaries. Methodism is well on its march to stardom in Christ Jesus.

Hebrews 10: 24-25 urges: "Let us be concerned for one another, to help one another, to show love and to do good. Let us not give up the habit of meeting together, as some are doing. Instead let us encourage one another all the more, since you see that the Day of the Lord is coming nearer." (TEV)

A vibrant church drills down its roots and like a tree sends out messages of love in the community through our volunteerism in its many programs of reaching out to the unchurched, disadvantaged, disenfranchised, physically challenged, homeless, and other individuals of society in need of physical and spiritual comfort.

Let us heed the call of John Wesley, who founded the Methodist movement, when he said: "The world is my parish." Emphasizing that our ministry and witness does not include just our community but beyond. A famous Methodist layman, Henry Denman, once stated: "We must help the local congregation to realize that the church must be the church. It is not a club, but the church is Christ living and working in the community. And by your witness in your jobs, vocations, and community involvement you extend the church's growth outward and upward. You will find that your witness you will experience what the early disciples learned and the whole city was favorable to them."

We are the modern equivalent of the verse in Acts 1:8. It reveals that "you shall be my witness in Jerusalem, and in all Judea and Samaria, and to the ends of the earth about my death and resurrection." (LB)

The implication of our witness is the fact that we proclaim our faith by our personal interaction with others. People bring people to the church. Acts 2:47 says: "The Lord added to their number daily those being saved." Our Christian religion is a movement of excitement and growth. Christ gives us the motivation, energy, and ability to get the gospel to our community and the world.

So my challenge is: How are you fitting into God's plan for expanding Christianity? What is your place in this movement?

Let's pray.

For the renewal of the Church.

Renew our Church, Lord,
Your people in this land,

Save us from cheap words
And self deception in your service.

In the power of your Spirit
Transform us, and shape us
By your cross.

Amen

12

FEAR NOT, I AM WITH YOU

Matt. 8:23-27

Good morning. There is a story of a teen ager who took a short cut on his way home through a cemetery one dark night and accidentally fell into a freshly dug grave. He tried several times to climb out but, finally, gave up and sat down in a corner to wait for morning. He fell asleep until another boy fell in and began trying to climb out. Then the first boy reached over and tapped the second boy on the shoulder and remarked: "Might as well keep company with me. I couldn't get out either!" Hearing the voice, the second boy was so frightened that, like a rocket, he made it six feet to the top of the grave.

Fear brings incredible power. Psychologists call it the adrenaline in us that pushes the body to do unexpected moves.

As a result of the terrorist attacks on September 11, 2001, many of us are fearful of our lives. The heightened alerts issued by Homeland Security continue to feed on our fear of the unknown. Many are afraid to fly. Many are afraid to go to big cities. Many are fearful to ride subway trains. Many avoid crowded places. Fortunately, here in Juneau, we don't have those kind of situations, except perhaps during tourist season.

There are people who are afraid of Middle Easterners, and many of them also fear for their lives. We fear terrorists. And during the Iraq war we were fearful that Saddam Hussein might unleash weapons of mass destruction. We are glad that it didn't happened. And that relieved many parents, spouses and kinfolks of soldiers who were in that battle. We also feared that the Iraq war would trigger a global war between the Muslims and the West, or between Islam and Christians. If such will be the case, millions of people will suffer and die.

Who among us has not experienced fear. Fear seems to be dominant in our hearts during these turbulent times. As religious leaders would describe it, it is our human existential situation. Fear is no respecter of persons, ages, positions, or places. To be human is to fear. We are vulnerable to fear—physically, emotionally, and spiritually.

But what does the Bible say about fear, and how to deal with fear? Let's turn to Jesus! We find that Jesus has something to teach us. Jesus warns us to live our lives with joy, love, and hope. Do you know that our Lord Jesus Christ often mentioned the words: "fear, troubled, anxious and afraid"?

Yet He assures us and with great assurance with these words: "Fear not! Do not be anxious! Let not your hearts be troubled, neither let them be afraid." Do not be afraid of anything. Not a single sparrow falls to the ground without your Father's consent. You are of more value than many sparrows. We are more precious than flowers or birds to be left out of the care and love of our Master and Savior.

The disciples knew what it was like to feel overwhelmed by fear. On the Sea of Galilee, as wind and waves battered their boat, they realized this was no ordinary storm. Their vessel was filling with water, and they fully expected to drown. Jesus was on the boat with them, yet somehow remained fast asleep. Reaching out in total desperation, they cried out to Him: "Lord, save us! We are perishing!" Only then did Jesus act to still the raging storm.

If the fears of those disciples were dispelled by the words of Jesus, who reassured them they have nothing to fear for their lives because they were in the presence of the Master of Life, how much more for us today when we need Him in our moments of fear, anxiety and uncertainty. We do believe that Jesus, who was on the Sea of Galilee is the same Jesus who is here with us today and tomorrow, reassuring us that He is in control of our lives, come what way, wherever we are and in whatever situation we are in. We have met Jesus Christ in our moments of joy and fear, and we know in our hearts we could rely on his words.

Thus it is many times with us when we face fear in any circumstance He seeks to calm the storm in our lives. As the Psalmist said: "Call upon Me in the day of trouble." Days of trouble. Hours of crisis. Moments of urgent and fearful need. They come to us all unexpectedly, like a thief in the night. How can we prepare for such times?

We can prepare to meet our fears by being ready to cry aloud to the Lord for his saving help, and boldly expecting His deliverance without doubt and in total confidence.

He tells us: "I will deliver you, and you shall glorify me." These are words of assurance. Who can doubt what that means in our life whenever we are troubled and face life-threatening events?

In the Philippines, Filipino boys and girls often hear of fearful objects—things that go bumping in the night like blood hungry semi-humans, ogres that dwell in trees, and witches that prey on little kids. But one particular creature of the night that I was most fearful of as a boy was the so-called *tikbalang* described as a half-horse and half-human being, who walks in the night, looking for young boys. Thus, like many boys of my age, I was deathly afraid of going out late at night alone. However, when I grew up I saw a sculpture of this supposed fearsome thing in Manila. Frankly, it was not really that bad. This tikbalang was just a figment of my imagination. You have to know the creature that you are afraid of, and you'll discover that you are a braver person than before.

Now what is fear? Fear is caused by an approaching danger. A psychologist describes it as an element of emotion, a part of our native equipment, and I might add it is God-given. Like any other normal emotion, it has a conservative, essential purpose. Our problem is not to get rid of fear, but how to use fear constructively.

For example: there is no animal without fear. For some animals, like the white tail deer and the rabbit, fear is the sole means of defence or escape. We have the same equipment in our human bodies, but in us, it is linked up with more than just part of our body. It is geared to our psyche or thinking process and our more complex emotional machinery.

Parents usually teach their children to be afraid of certain things as they grow up. As parents, we want our children to be afraid of playing with matches or lighters, with rusty nails, playing in the busy streets, and drinking unknown liquids out of bottles. Even not to talk to strangers. These are healthy fears. And we adults are motivated by fears every day of our lives and moved by fear. We do many good and constructive things such as lock the door at night, buy life or fire insurance, pay the necessary taxes, and so forth. But we all agree that fear is an emotion of extremely high voltage, and it can become a destructive and disintegrating force.

In the interview of many dying people, the number one top fear is fear of the unknown. That is understandable. As a rule, we are not afraid of a thing when we know what the thing is, like the tikbalang I mentioned. You have heard the saying "leap in the dark." Some people fear the dark. That includes me. Why? Because we don't know what it is or can get hurt. We do not understand its sounds and shadows. Even the Psalmist David feared darkness as he expressed his feelings in Psalm 88 with these words: "my companion as become darkness, there is only darkness everywhere, my acquaintances are in darkness."

In Masonry, a candidate is brought from darkness into light. Light makes a difference. The candidate begins to see what his life was and what his life is going to be in the light of the principles of freemasonry. The darkness that shrouded his mind about life becomes clearer as the candidate is brought to the full light of things unknown to him before. This is what St. Paul in I Corinthians 13: 11-13: "When I was a child I spoke like a child, I thought like a child. I reasoned like a child; when I became an adult I put an end to childish ways, for now we see in a mirror, dimly, but then we will see face to face. Now I know only in part, then I know fully,even as I have been fully known?" When darkness is cleared away, then our fears will fade away.

It is important for us to know that many of our irrational fears are rooted in some past experiences, in some hidden dread buried deep in the darkness of our unconscious minds,

Let me tell you the story of a man, who went to see a psychiatrist, because he was having problems sleeping. He heard voices speaking in the night. "What do the voices say"" asked the psychiatrist. "They say, is he asleep yet?" Well, after a great deal of digging into the memories of past events in the man's life, he finally remembered that those were the last words that he heard from the surgeon say just before he underwent surgery several years ago. "Is he asleep het?"

So once the fear was dragged out into the light and examined. the fear was dispelled and the man was able to sleep once more,

So what are we to do with fear? The famous preacher Norman Vincent Peale once urged: "Don't settle down and live permanently with your fears. If you do, you will never be happy and effective." How true! How can we lead an effective life if we are demoralized and paralyzed because of fear. Even as our country tries to cope with terrorism, most of us known intuitively that living in fear is not living at all.

I can think of no better cure for fear than our faith in Jesus Christ. Jesus is concerned about our fears. In the story of Jesus walking on the sea, the disciples were afraid and Jesus said to then: "Have no fear!"

On the Mount of Transfiguration when Jesus came down His face shown brightly and the disciples were afraid. Jesus confronted them! "Rise and have no fear." Incredible as it seems. The Creator of the Universe desires us to take His words in total confidence in our moments of fear, anxiety and trouble. The right step toward experiencing God's powerful promise is simply to cry out in fervent appeal for help when we are in the grip of fear, To paraphrase His words: "call "upon Me when you are afraid and I will deliver you, and you wlll glorify me."

Let's look at once more Biblical readings when crying to God for deliverance in our moments of fear. One of my favorites is this one." They that wait upon the Lord shall renew their strength. They shall mount up with wings as eagles, they shall walk and not be weary, and they shall run and not faint."

Then do you remember the official who went up to Jesus in the synagogue and told Him that his daughter had died? Jesus replied: "Do not fear, only believe!"

Have no fear. Fear not. Do not be afraid. Jesus reassures us: "I am with you always till the end of the age." Jesus is trying to comfort us in the midst of our national and personal fears. God loves us so much that He will never abandon us. What a reassurance. I can live with that, and I hope you can to.

Let me end my message with a personal experience with fear. Years ago I was returning to the Philippines after my graduate studies at Syracuse University on board a huge cargo-liner. After weeks at sea we were in the middle of the Pacific Ocean in what sailors call a "potato patch," the most turbulent expanse of the Pacific ocean. Our ship was buffeted by twenty-foot waves and made our vessel like a cork bobbing up and down. All of us twelve passengers huddled in the mess hall and were gripped with fear. Every one of us were saying our deepest prayers for deliverance. Our faces were bathed in tears. In a couple of days of these vicious buffeting by the waves, the good ship captain, a bearded Norwegian, appeared in the mess hall, and announced with authority that our good ship is weathering the storm, engines are running well, and that we should be safely beyond the storm at the end of the day. And it happened. We made it safely to our destination. For me it was Manila. Fear of dying at sea was imminent at that time. Our prayers calmed our nerves. God was in control of our lives.

The greatest need of our country today is to take a long and hard look at the face of the Great Architect of the Universe. Then we will know that God is still the

Master of our lives. God is still the Lord of history. God is still the Hope of our society, our nation, and our world. God is in control of our lives today and tomorrow.

Martin Luther once said: "I know not the way He leads me, but well I do know my Guide. What have I to fear?"

Can you confidently proclaim; "What have I to fear?"

In our fears, God is with us in Jesus Christ.

Let's pray.

Almighty God and Heavenly Father, who through thy son Jesus Christ has given us the assurance to take your words "Fear not, I'm with you" in absolute confidence in our moments of fear, distress and trouble, we ask you to deliver us from any situations which threaten our daily existence so that we may glorify and praise your loving kindness. May we leave this sanctuary with courage and your abundant blessings to face the world knowing that you are with us always even to the end of the age.

Amen

13

PRAYERS, PRESENCE, GIFTS, AND SERVICE

2 Corinthians 9: 6-15

Welcome to our worship service today. And welcome to the greatest institution we can belong on earth, the church. This is not a man-made institution like the Rotarians, Kiwanis, Masonry, and so forth. The church is a divine institution which is rooted deep in the Body of Christ. We who are here today are part of this Body of Christ.

As you know the church has many branches known as Protestants, Roman Catholics, Orthodox, and so forth. But, let me speak of the United Methodist Church with which I am familiar. The UMC was founded by John Wesley whose teachings are the basis of our church doctrines, discipline and rituals. The Methodists are not only the followers of John Wesley. There are the Wesleyans, African Methodists, Methodist Protestants, and Evangelical United Brethren, some of whom merged several decades ago. All of these churches trace their roots to John Wesley.

These churches look back to the Aldersgate experience of John Wesley. This incident took place in 1738 commonly referred to as the famous heart warming experience. One night John Wesley was attending a prayer meeting of the Moravians at Aldersgate in London. The preacher was expounding on the epistle of John. Suddenly Wesley felt his "heart strangely warmed." These are his words as recorded in his journal: "I felt I did trust in Christ. Christ alone for salvation, and an assurance was given me that he had taken away my sins, even mine, and saved me from the law of sin and death."

Up to this point of his religious life, Wesley's greatest fear was about death. He was afraid that he was going to hell. As an Anglican priest he had been preaching the Word of God but he was not sure of his message. Aldersgate was the tipping point of his ministry, and England was never the same. His powerful messages of love and salvation to the masses of 18th century England eventually led to the formation of a society called Methodists, because he was so methodical in his preaching that society became a church when Wesley's followers came to America.

When you join a church you are asked to make a vow. This vow is recited before the congregation to signify the formality of joining the church. In the United Methodist Church you make this vow when you are baptized, accepted on a profession of faith or transferred to another congregation.

This vow is stated in a question as follows: "Will you be loyal to the church, uphold it by your prayers, your presence, your gifts, and your service?"

And the response is: "I will."

This vow is your obligation. Your promise to the church. The key words are prayers, presence, gifts and service. These are not merely words. These are action words which clearly spell our obligations as members of the church. Every time a member is received, baptized or transferred we renew our vows. If a child is baptized, adults make the promises for them.

Let me explain why we as Christians need to be reminded of our obligations and their importance in our personal lives as we struggle on our faith journey.

We do many things by faith. I'm not talking about faith in your car, faith in your bank, faith in your doctor and so forth. I'm talking about faith in God. We petition God for many things for ourselves, families, children, friends, and many others. We are not assured of the outcome of our prayers. No matter how hard we knock on the door and no matter how deeply we pray, there is no assurance that whatever we asked in the name of the Lord will happen. We entrust our petitions to God in faith. That is all we can do.

When I was in high school in the Philippines, I prayed to God to send me to the United States to study. I kept on praying to God for this petition. I went to college and nothing happened. But, I kept up my prayers. I envied some of my classmates who went to America on their own resources or were awarded scholarships. Nevertheless, I did not lose faith in the goodness of God. I kept up my youthful dreams and hopes. And then one day I received a letter from the American Embassy in Manila requesting me to report to the embassy for an interview regarding my application for a Fulbright scholarship. Wow! I was interviewed, and a week later I was informed that I was chosen to receive a Fulbright scholarship for graduate study at Northwestern University.

Does God answer prayers? You bet He does. At least from my experience. I must submit, however, that God does not answer all prayers. But for some experiences in my life and my family I know He answers prayers. The waiting maybe agonizing, frustrating still, if we have faith "all things work together for good to them that love the Lord."

There are two types of prayers that we offer to God. The first one is the corporate prayer. This is the prayer offered by a collective body of believers in this house of worship. It is the prayer which we all join through our minister as he or she offers the thanksgiving or praise and petition for God's help for our problems, hopes, and concerns. Our corporate prayer reaches the throne of God, and miracles happen in the lives of individuals, institutions, the nation, and the world.

My family believes in the power of corporate prayer. When we were living in Arkansas one of our daughters had a serious medical problem. Our family doctor recommended immediate surgery. Meantime our minister prayed for her during the worship service. Her Sunday School classmates and youth group sent their prayers to God. When the appointed time for surgery came, the surgeon made a final check on her condition. Ex-ray plates were examined, blood test made, and even an exploratory probe into her abdomen was done. The results showed that there was no suspected tumor. She was sent home with a clean bill of health. We rejoiced in miracles wrought by the power of corporate prayer.

The second type of prayer is our individual prayer. Our personal meditation or dialogue with God. Whether we do this action in the privacy our room, behind our desk, or behind the wheel while driving to work, the place does not matter. Again whether we do our prayers orally or mentally the method is not important. What is important is that we communicate our inner most thoughts, longings, petitions, wants and thanksgiving to God. In these brief moments we try to connect our souls to God. God cannot come into our hearts unless we open the dialogue with Him. We have to plug our hearts to the source of divine power, and that is God.

The second part of our obligation is **presence.** Obviously, we cannot develop and grow in faith without our presence in corporate worship, and faith building activities of our church. As Christians we have not fully arrived. We are still learning what faith is all about. Our attendance in corporate worship is vital to our Christian growth. As John Wesley said: "We are still on the road to perfection." To be perfect in our faith we must exert every effort to participate in activities and ministries of the church. Your presence in this communion service strengthens your faith in a loving and merciful God.

When we served as counselors at Eagle River Methodist camp in Juneau, AK our morning meditation leader pointed out why presence is fundamental to our Christian growth. We had a fire place in the lodge. Attention was riveted on the blazing pine logs which are giving off much warmth. Our speaker pulled one small burning log and laid it aside. The flame fizzled out and the lonely log was just a smoking ember, and was not giving off warmth at all. Our speaker said: "This is what happens when we are not involved in the work and ministry of the church."

Although we can commune with God in the woods, or while we are fishing, there is no substitute for being in corporate worship. When we are alone we lose our glow. We lose our strength. We become lonely. Our faith shrivels just like that smoking useless pine log.

Hence, our presence in worship and ministry of our church is absolutely necessary in our faith journey. That includes our presence in committee meetings, for which we United Methodists are noted. Never deprive the community of the gift of your presence. You are important in the Body of Christ.

And the third obligation where we need to comply if we are to be worthy members of the Body of Christ is the **giving of gifts.** I think sometimes this is the most difficult and delicate to handle, because this is connected with our money and resources. It is easy for a millionaire to give money. But, for the rest of us we have to consider our monthly bills, college expenses, replacement of carpets, braces for our children and so forth.

We have a hundred ways to spend money. To tithe and give a portion of our income to the church, that is another matter. And yet there is no escaping of the fact that the church needs money to run its many program and ministries and to keep it a viable and transforming institution.

When we give money to a cause we often ask question: "What is in it for me?" In other words, what do I get out of my dollar? Have you ever thought about what you get out of your money from the church? We can spend a lot of time on what the church can do for you, but let me ask you a question. Can you buy peace of mind, trust and faith in God, wholesome fellowship with Christians, and love or support from members? Can you buy the love of God?

There is no monetary value for these things. Our response is to give our rightful share of what God has given to us. This is stewardship. We give not because we are obligated, or because of a sense of duty. We give out of a joyful heart. God loves a cheerful giver.

In Second Corinthians 9 verses 11 and 12, St. Paul tells us: "He will always make you rich enough to be generous at all times, so that many will thank God for your gifts which they receive from us. For this service you perform not only meet the needs of God's people, but also produces an outpouring of grateful thanks to God."

But, there is another aspect of gifts. This is our **time** and **talent.** Time is another difficult gift to consider. Either we have plenty of time to do something or we don't. It all depends on our priorities in life. That also depends in our life work or vocation. We work forty some hours a week, Monday to Friday. That leaves plenty of time on weekends to engage in our sports, or whatever things we loved to use our weekend hours.

When we are requested to teach Sunday School, lead a fund raising program, or do other church activities, do you respond: "I have no time. I'm sorry, I'm too busy with my project at home." Are you too busy pursuing wealth and pleasure and neglecting your church work?

We can give a hundred excuses to get us off the hook. Also remember the next time you are about to turn down a chance to serve, think twice. You may be denying others of your gifts.

God has given all of us gifts or talents. Our talents or abilities vary a lot. This is our inner most quality which qualified us for our jobs, or whatever. Some are gifted with leadership, writing skill, singing voice, speaking ability, and so forth. Or some are gifted with strong arms, good listening ears, expert counseling and the like. Whatever it is, use these talents, abilities and strengths for God's work. And why not look for these gifts and talents in others and praise them. It will brighten their lives and yours for the glory of God. As St. Paul says in his letter to the Romans: "God has given each of us the ability to do *certain* things well." (Romans 12: 6 LB).

St. Paul advised Timothy: "Do not neglect the gift that is in you." And Timothy used his talent of speaking effectively to spread he Word of God."

Now I come to the last part of our obligation. Good churchmanship require **service** which is tied up with our gifts, talents and abilities. Our gifts of money and resources are not any good if they are not followed with what we can do. Sometimes we grumble, I have already given, what more can I do? Yes, there is more to do and that is service. Working for God is unending. Your service for God's cause, ministries, programs of the Body of Christ is urgently needed.

The Bible says in James 2:26 that "Faith without works is dead." I equate work as service. We have to show action in our faith through service. We have to show evidence of our faith. Service is faith in action. Your involvement in the ministry of the church makes a big difference in its success or failure.

When our youngest daughter Mutya (Mae) was a freshman in college, she joined her youth group for a two-week summer service in Appalachia, eastern Kentucky, to work among the impoverish mountain folks. She served for two summers, digging ditches, building outhouses, repairing broken down houses, and distributing clothes and food. Having come from a well sheltered life her Appalachian summer work gave her a first hand experience in the pitiful social and economic conditions of Appalachians.

When she came home she told us stories of grinding poverty and lonely isolation of the people. They did not only need food, clothing, and shelter. They needed somebody to talk with them and to tell them about the love of God. Out of this experience she developed her vocation. That of a social worker. She is now the social worker of Jefferson County in Fairfield, Iowa.

She and her husband are very much involved in their church mission and ministry. They have two beautiful daughters, Chelsea and Samantha, our pride and joy.

As Christians we cannot be couch potatoes or Monday morning quarter backs. We have to pitch in and get involved in the life and mission of the church. Christianity is not a spectator sport.

Do you now realize that to be a member of the church requires an awesome sense of responsibility? The church of Christ challenges us every day to a life of prayer, presence, gifts and service.

Let us pray:

Almighty and Ever loving God we pray that You will give us the strength and faith to carry out our obligations so that we may serve You with all our hearts and soul. Amen.

14

MINISTRY OF THE PRESENCE

Mark 1:16-20; Matt. 13: 47-50

Before I begin my brief message this morning, Cora and I would like to express our deepest thanks for your expression of love and care during our darkest moments of grief. Our beloved daughter Lualhati (Lulu) G. Schenk passed away on Oct. 8, 2001 and left a grieving, devoted husband and three handsome boys and all of us. Your cards of condolence, prayers, e mails, plants and flowers provided great comfort and helped wipe away our tears of sorrow.

We believe that our daughter is in heaven, where there is no more pain, sickness and death, and where she lives eternally with our Savior and Lord.

Cora and I are so happy that we are with you to express how you have helped us pass through the valley of the shadow of death. As King David said in Psalm 23: "Your goodness and unfailing kindness shall be with us all of our life."

As most of you know we have been traveling to Douglas Church, and this visit will be our 8th time which includes a 1997 stay for a book signing and a 1998 VIM team when we were here to work on the parsonage. The rest of our visits were devoted to our Filipino-American ministry work.

This program started when I was the president of the National Association of Filipino American United Methodists. Our national objective then was the development of ethnic congregations. This was in keeping with the 1984 quadrennial emphasis of the General Conference of the United Methodist Church.

I just happened to be in the right position at the right time. Our organization started this new congregational development program in California, Missouri, Illinois, Texas, New Jersey, and New York. Many volunteers were involved, mostly laymen and women, who went out looking for Filipinos and gathered them in small fellowship groups, and eventually some of them became worshipping congregations. I recorded the history of some of these new congregations in my book *Churches Aflame*, a History of Asian American United Methodist Churches, published by Abingdon Press, which came out in 1996. Included in this book are also the history of new churches of the Koreans, Chinese, Japanese, Taiwanese and Indians written by their historians.

At that time I was also a member of the General Commission of Archives and History. And there's where I met Bea Shepard, a fellow historian and the only Alaskan I ever met. During our first meeting in Madison, New Jersey, I asked her in my naivete about the famous Eskimo delicacy called "muktuk" and requested her to bring some next time we meet. She said muktuk is not found in Juneau, but there are other interesting things in the area. There are lots of Filipinos. She invited me to come over and check the possibilities of a Filipino ministry. What a coincidence. I said that's exactly what our national organization was interested in. Hence, Cora and I have come here on the invitation of Bea Shepard and the church. This program of the Ministry of the Presence was originally presented to the Board of Global Ministries, and later assigned a funding number. Since our national organization started this program in 1984 there are now 29 Filipino American United Methodist Churches in the U.S., the majority being in California and Texas. The program is still going in these states and in other states like in Illinois, Missouri, Virginia, and New York.

As I described the development of these churches in my book, many of these newly formed churches did not grow overnight. Many of them are the result of sacrifice, and hard work by many devoted Filipino and American laymen and women, and pastors. They struggled against discrimination, funding shortages, hostility, indifference, politics in our church. But they persevered and like I described in the title of my article "Gathering the Scattered" these scattered blossomed into worshipping congregations. These churches were the fruit of the Holy Spirit who guided the men and women to the harvest fields.

Moreover, speaking about the growth of ethnic United Methodist churches, the fastest growing ones are the Koreans. In most cities in the U.S. you will find Korean UMCs. Today there are some 600 Methodist Korean churches. They have their own district superintendents, and even a bishop. Most Koreans in the US are Protestants because of the early work of American missionaries in South Korea. The largest Methodist Church in the world is in Seoul. It has a membership of 30,000 people. Its founder and former minister is Sundoo Kim, who is now one of the bishops of the UMC. He is dynamic person and perhaps the finest preacher in Korea. The church has missionaries in Russia, Philippines, and other parts of the world. Astounding, indeed.

Now let me go to my main message today—the Ministry of the Presence. During my first sermon in 1992 I described it, but I bet that many of you probably wouldn't remember the points of that sermon. So I figured they are worth telling again. I remember that if a message of a preacher can be recalled a week after he delivered it, then he must be pretty good. I do not claim that goodness. Our pastor in Cedar Falls, Iowa, has a sermon outline which is printed in the bulletin and some blank spaces for us to fill in the points. I think that technique works well in recall studies.

Our Cedar Falls church has a mission statement: To glorify God by making disciples for Jesus Christ." In other words, we the congregation are the ministers and are commissioned to carry the message of love and faith in our places of work, and wherever we are.

In the Ministry of the Presence, there are three steps or components, which we follow in our work: we call, we tell, and we invite.

We call which means we identify our subject. This is the who. Who are the potentials: the kind of people we would like to call on. This is where our scripture reading comes in. It is about fishing for fish and men. Now the fishing place is the Sea of Galilee. Although called the sea, it's really a big lake of fresh water, fed by various northern springs and eventually becomes the River Jordan. During the time of Jesus, the Sea of Galilee was teeming with fish. Fish is the mainstay of the daily diet of the Israelis and Palestinians, especially those who lived by the shore. Along the shore lived many commercial fishermen like Simon Peter and John, the Zebedee brothers. They used nets to catch fish. Some used barb hooks. I found out in my research that they used the barb hooks to snag fish. Wow, that's what I do at DIPAC.

The early Palestinian fishermen caught many kinds of fish which they called "clean (good) and uncleaned (bad) fish." According to my research, the clean fish are what they call Peter's fish, after Peter, and like sardine. In my readings I found out that Peter's fish is called "tilapia" which is found today in Asia, like in the Philippines, sold at Fred Meyers, and even in Iowa. This is a prolific fish. In six months, tilapia can grow to two marketable pounds. A friend who was on pilgrimage to the Holy Land tasted this fish, broiled on charcoal, like Jesus must have had, for breakfast with the fishermen. He said the fish was delicious. The clean fish are sold to the Jews and Palestinians. The unclean fish (bad) are the catfish, eels, and lamprey. These are sold to the non-Jews or to the Gentiles or perhaps to the Samaritans. In Iowa catfish is a clean fish. We eat them, deep fried and are delicious.

Now what is the relationship of fishing to our Ministry of the Presence? By now it is obvious that fishing is calling on people, meeting all kinds of people in their places of work, homes and other places. Our most productive meetings were at DIPAC, Fred Meyers, Filipino Community Center, and on Franklin street. Peter's fish are found in the homes of those who spoke our language—Ilocano and Tagalog. It is surprising that the word gets around of our visits, so one visit will lead to another, and so we built a core of friends and acquaintances. This then led to a number of personal Bible study meetings with some elderly Filipinos, senior citizens. A couple of them have died, but I was able to lead them to the basis of the Christian faith—which is faith in Jesus Christ as Savior and Lord. Some of them didn't know the Lord's Prayer as they didn't learned it in the Philippines.

When a call is made on a person, or family, who is receptive—the good fish—we go out to the next phase, telling them of the Good News. We simply talked to them about the importance of their spiritual life. Some of our visits we discover that many of them have not been to church. Most of our Filipino people here are Roman Catholics. But many are nominal Catholics. That is they are in church only during baptisms and religious holiday days. The reason they give why they have not been to church is that they worked for a living, that is, they have very little time to spend on the spiritual side. Also, when they have time to spare they used it for sports and part time jobs.

As you know we are enveloped in a culture of materialism. This is not only true in the USA but all over the world. And many Filipinos are hooked in this culture. I'm not saying that it's bad to pursue a life of comfort and luxuriate in the bounties of living in America. But when this becomes a magnificent obsession at the expense of our spiritual life then we fall by the wayside. We might miss the heavenly train, and that train makes only one stop. If we fail to heed the Word of God on earth, then there is no other stops left. When we knock at the portal of heaven and Jesus asks us "Why should I let you to my heaven?" What's your answer? You might reply that I went to church regularly, attended Sunday School, gave food to the poor, said my prayers, etc.

My friends, those answers are not good enough to get you to heaven. We are not saved by our works, but our faith in Jesus Christ as our works are never complete. We blew it at times.

I think Attorney General John Ashcroft, who is a devoted evangelical, states our situation this way in his book *On My Honor*: "We have more money but less virtue. We have more of the things disposable and less of the things eternal. We must learn to give. We will find something far more valuable than money we so vainly strive after and so tenaciously cling to."

Paul in his letter to the Hebrews 13: 5 writes: "Keep your lives free from the love of money, and be satisfied with what you have. For God has said, "I will never leave you. I will never abandon you"

Third point in the Ministry of the Presence, after we made the call and tell our story, the next step part is the action. We invite them to church. Or advise them to go to the church of their choice. We do not seek conversion. We remind people about their religious obligations.

Let me share an experience. On our way to Juneau on Alaska Airline, I was seated beside a middle age Filipino who was on his way to Ketchikan. He worked as a foreman at a fish cannery. I told him we were on our way to Juneau to work on the Filipino-American Ministry of Douglas Community United Methodist Church. He was curious what this ministry is all about. He admitted that he was a Roman Catholic and familiar with the rituals of his church, but he did not know much of the tenets of his faith. He finally confessed that he does not have faith at all. He said he was saddened by what he has been reading and hearing about pedophile priests. He has lost confidence in the leadership of his church. I told him that the church will still be there when he is ready to return. The church is eternal but its personnel are ephemeral.

And to shore up his waning faith I quoted my favorite verse John 3:16. A verse I grew with up as a child of a Methodist minister in the Philippines. *"For God so loved the world that he gave his only begotten son that whosoever believes in him should not perish but have eternal life."*

My new found acquaintance was astonished to hear those words. I stated that this verse is found in the New Testament. He said he has never read the Bible. I replied that I can arrange to send him a Bible. That Bible with my dedication is now in his hands courtesy of the Douglas CUMC. I hoped and prayed that I planted the seeds of the Good News.

Now, the important part of the invitation is that the person comes to church. He or she is warmly welcomed by any member and the pastor. I taught public relations at the university and the basic of PR is to make your customer happy. In church this job is not only the pastor's, but more importantly the job of members. As you all know it is so nice when somebody welcomes you, gives you a genuine smile and talks to you. Shake our hands and more smile. Yes, extend the warm hands fellowship. Say nice things how wonderful of you to visit our church. Then invite them to come again. Tell them our church is a caring and loving congregation. A visitor or guest who comes to the church should leave with a good feeling and positive impression of the people and the church.

We distinctly remember when we first met Leroy and Sandie Coon. I was in the computer room fiddling around with the computer. He said "Art it's so nice that you and Cora are here. Welcome." His smile was the brightest and sincerest I have ever seen. He extended a firm hand shake. He continues to show that bright smile of welcome to this day.

Cora and I attended another church last Sunday in Juneau. Printed on their bulletin were the words "Visitors are welcomed." We went to the church to follow up with some of the Filipinos we have earlier visited. But before and after the worship service, it seemed we were strangers from another planet. No word of welcome from the minister as he made the announcements of church programs. When we left the church not one member or the pastor gave us a smile or a handshake. We suffered an awful feeling of unwelcomeness.

Last Sunday, we shook hands with a Black couple who were worshipping for the first time in our church. Not one of the members came out to greet them. This is not an isolated case. We have seen this happen in other Methodist churches in California, Arkansas, Iowa, Minnesota and Ohio.

Hence, we Methodists have a practice of greeting members and visitors before our divine service begins. We do not take fellow worshippers for granted. Our smiles and hand of fellowship are shown as a warm welcome in the Body of Christ, the church, And half hearted smiles and limp hands won't cut it.

In Revelation 3:20 God urges: "Listen I stand at the door and knock. If any one hears my voice and opens the door, I will come into his house, and eat with him, and he will eat with me."

Let's pray.

Almighty and Loving God, who through your son Jesus Christ called us to be your witnesses, grant us grace and power to carry your message of hope and salvation to your people in this community. Amen.

15

PARABLES AND FOLK TALES

Matt: 18: 1-5; 19: 13:13-15
Mark 4: 10-20

My sermon today is a combination of Sunday School and old fashioned college lecture about folk lore and the parables of Jesus. This is a subject which intrigued me after writing my book *Tales From the 7,000 Isles.* Is there a connection or relationship between the two, 'folk lore and parable?' Is there a Christian perspective to folk lore, just as Jesus used the parable in driving home the hard truth of Christian life?

After listening to this sermon, I would leave the answer to you. That is if you are still stay with me for the next 20 minutes. Cora warned me earlier to keep in mind the KISS principle on public speaking. Keep it short sweetheart.

Parables are the best known stories Jesus told in His sermons. Why did Jesus used parables? He used them to open the minds of men and women of some parts of God's truth. Parable is another name for fable, as in Aesop fables. Unlike the Aesop fables, the characters in the parables are people or plants. There are no animals which are the favorite subject in fables.

We have heard the parables since we were in Sunday School. Parables have been described as "earthly story with a heavenly meaning." Also it is an earthly story that reveals a reality which is breaking in upon human experience. The parables in the New Testament with which we are quite familiar have their historical origin in the Old Testament. Jesus extensively used the parables as a teaching method in his ministry.

There are 46 parables in the New Testament. Each of them is a sermon by itself. And Jesus always end the parables with these words: "Go and do likewise."

Jewish priests are familiar with teaching points of the parables. Parables are also a favorite method of teachers. There are parables in the Old Testament. Most are in 2 Samuel 12: 1-7. David coveted Bathsheba, the wife of Uriah and in order to gain possession of her he deliberately arranged to have Uriah sent to his death. David was quite unaware that he had done anything wrong, after all, he was the king. So Nathan came to David and told a simple story.

"There were two men who lived in a certain city. One was rich and had flocks of sheep in abundance and all that his heart could desire. The other was a poor man, who possessed one ewe lamb which was so dear to him that it was almost as one of his family. A friend came to visit the rich man and he didn't like to take one of his numerous flocks to set a meal before him, so he took and slaughtered the ewe lamb which was all that the poor man had."

David was a generous soul, and the story kindled his heart. He was mad at the rich man. Then David asked Nathan: "Tell me who that man was. I swear that he will die for this and before he dies he will pay that poor man four times of what he took."

Nathan's answer hit squarely in the eyes, "You are the man."

That was a parable to open the King's eyes.

The Old Testament parable has three identifying marks or characteristics. These identifying marks also apply to other Old Testament parables and to the New Testament parables.

A parable is secular, that is non-religious and its content and characterization are familiar items. Like a poor man and his only beloved possession, a ewe lamb, a common characteristic in Israel.

A parable is a simile or metaphor. A metaphor is a figure of speech in which one object is likened to another by speaking of it as if it were that other, e.g. a rich man is likened to King David. A metaphor's comparison as "like or as" but not explicitly. However, in a simile words of comparison "like or as" is made explicit.

Like the parable about the poor and rich man, there is another striking parable in the Old Testament which makes use of the metaphor. This is Jotham's parable of the trees. Jotham compared the 70 sons of Gideon as the trees, and the thorn bush as Abimelech. The fruitful trees could produce good fruits and the thorn bush would catch fire and burn. Abimelech was the thorn bush and was destroyed.

The word parable is a Greek word which means simply "to throw beside" or to compare two objects which are thrown beside each other. So when two objects are thrown beside each other, i. e. compared, it causes the mind and the imagination to struggle with reality which is being disclosed. The metaphor produces the insight and understanding. This means our mind are challenged to see the connection between the characters and every day experience.

Parables used vivid language and economy of words. These may have been real events in real villages inhabited by real people. David coveted Bathsheba. David is the rich man. Bathsheba is the ewe lamb. In the New Testament, Jesus gives a pictorial description of the bearing and posture of the cheating publican or tax collector, who was humble and repentant. The Pharisee was described as proud and self-righteous. The picture of a humble and repentant man is contrasted with the picture of a proud and self-righteous man.

Parables involve the hearer as a participant. Nathan tells the story to David who is the object of the story. Jesus tells his parables before a live audience and addresses the story directly to His listeners.

The parable calls for a decision. David declares punishment for that man who took the ewe lamb that man will replace the ewe lamb and then will die. As in the New Testament parables, Jesus says at the conclusion: Go and do likewise. That is a decision for every man or woman to make after listening to each parable. From what I have read about the parables of Jesus He used themes which are prevalent in the region or in Israel.

For instance there is the folklore of the buried treasure such as jewels, gold and valuable trinkets. Every Jew entertains the fond hope of discovering such buried treasure. Palestine is placed in between Mesopotamia and Egypt, and thus had been on the route of caravans and invading armies which left behind treasures buried in the desert in those days, the most secure way to hide treasure was to bury it. This is precisely what one servant in the parable of the talent did. He buried the money in the ground. Unlike the others who received money they invested the money which earned more for their master. The 46 parables of Jesus are found in three gospels. Mark, Matthew and Luke record some of the similar parables. For instance the three gospels carry the parables of the sower, mustard seed, fig tree, and the wicked tenants with which we are all familiar. And as a growing boy in Sunday School in the Philippines I learned the stories by heart because of the moral lesson. Then there are similar parables carried by Matthew and Luke such as the faithful and wise servants, the talents, the house and kingdom divided. The strong man's house, and the return of the evil spirits.

Now that we understand the nature of the parables, let me lead you to their connection with folklores or folk tales so we can see their value and relevance to us.

There is a close similarity of parables and folk tales. Folk tales are taught in public schools in the Philippines. It is part of the curriculum in elementary schools. Grade school children learned their folk tales, although many of them learn some of the popular folk tales from their parents and grandparents. My mom was a great story teller of Filipino folk lores. Story telling is very much a part in the childhood of Filipino children and a vital part of our culture.

Story telling not only preserves the culture of a country, but also develops the foundation of values in society. Folk tales are a rich source of cultural values which remain with the child as he or she grows up.

As I mentioned, Jesus used parables to open the minds of His listeners about religious truths. In the same manner, folk tales are used to open the imagination of the child about the wonders of his environment. Usually the wonders about supernatural beings and phenomena.

Here are some characteristics of folk tales as used in behavioral control and value formation.

1. Folk lore provides amusement value. It provides humor. And humor is one of the way to develop a child's appreciation of the funny situations in life. Behind the humor, however, is a grain of wisdom, some teaching lesson about the follies of life, or the stupidity of certain behavior. Example is the "Buffalo and the Turtle" in my folk tale book. The buffalo or carabao in this folk tale is arrogant or boastful of his size and strength. He wouldn't even consider racing with anybody in the animal kingdom, much less to a lowly turtle. Well, the arrogant and boastful buffalo was humiliated in the race by means of a scheme. He worked out with his fellow turtles. The lesson here is that no one should be arrogant and boastful of anything because he or she will fall someday.

2. Folk lore has educational function. This function is clearly demonstrated in non-literate societies where people are used to listening or hearing rather than reading. In Ifugao and Tinguian societies in the

Philippines where they used folk lore as educational tool to teach children about the origins of life on earth, suns and stars, or spectacular phenomena such as comets and meteors. Since folklore is transmitted by oral communication, it plays a major role in transmitting and preserving social values. An example is the folk tale "Magno and the Magic Jar." Here we have a genie just like in the movie Aladdin. He is a kindly genie and gave Magno all the wishes he made. There are some fearsome episodes in the story, but as you relate this story the child becomes aware of places in the environment that he or she should not explore.

More importantly, reading our folk tales develops positive attitudes such as diligence, honesty and industry. Negative attitudes such as laziness, rebelliousness, snobbishness, and greed are ridiculed. And at the same time our folk tales are vehicles of prudence, courtesy and consideration. An example would be the tale of "Bindoy and the Greedy Boy." The title of this folk tale alone is a giveaway of the nature of this boy. Bindoy is a lazy and greedy boy. He is very selfish and thought only of himself. He did not share his food with his poor, starving mother, until one day he learned his lesson. He met an aswang or vampire. After that blood curdling incident Bindoy became a good boy.

3. Folk tales contribute to the maintenance of accepted patterns of behavior. Folk lore is a dynamic and enforcer of traditions. For Filipino kids who grow up in America they are missing a great deal of our social and cultural traditions that we Filipinos of the first generation have grown up with. For instance, respect for elders, courtesy in all aspects and reverence of wisdom and education are some of the traditional values that we parents fail to inculcate in our American born or raised children. It is a dream of every Filipino family to see that their children get a higher education and become professionals. Whether poor or rich, parents encourage or push their children to obtain a college degree. When I went home, after my graduate studies in the U.S, to visit my hometown Guimba, Nueva Ecija, I was amazed to see sign boards hanging outside the windows in many homes proclaiming that their children are lawyers, doctors, engineers, certified public accountants, pharmacists, and professors.

In America the situation is different. Recently, I read the pitiful story of a sixteen year old Filipina in San Francisco. Her parents worked on two jobs to keep up with her material needs. Care for their children was largely left in the hands of a baby-sitter. As the child grew up they gave all the material things to her, and they thought they were doing a great parenting job. Reality hit them hard when Carole turned 17 and dropped the bombshell. She was pregnant, and her baby's father had disappeared. The parents were devastated but assured their daughter that they would support her and her baby. A few weeks later Carole ran away from home. And last time the parents heard that Carole had an abortion.

Suddenly the American dream of this couple, like most Filipino parents have before coming to America, crashed and turned into a disaster. Would this have been prevented?

Of course, if you hear Dr. James Dobson, a popular TV family speaker. He says that most parents neglect to spend quality time with their growing children, and thus children grow up with less discipline and more permissiveness. You and I as parents have an obligation to our children to spend quality time with them. And one of the best ways to relate to our children is reading to them our popular folk tales, which like the parables of Jesus are guidelines to value formation.

Let me illustrate this function of folk lore by citing the Philippine social value system.

Deep in the psyche of a Filipino is the social-cultural value of hiya or shame. Our concept of hiya is not guilt or sin. Rather hiya is more of saving one's face or honor. This is a very powerful social deterrent in our society. The social implications of hiya is far reaching. We often say, "What you have done or said are shameful." Hiya or shame is connected with two other social values which are debt of gratitude and group cooperation or camaraderie.

These three social-cultural values are: shame, debt of gratitude and group cooperation define inter-personal relationship and ritual kinship in Philippine society. This relationship still prevails in our Filipino-American environment. Violations of these values mean the perpetrators incur social disfavor or lose face or are shunned.

These values are not taught. We teach these values more by our actions than from our words. Hence, our American friends wonder why we Filipinos behave as we do in this society. It is difficult for them to comprehend the concept of shame, debt of gratitude and group cooperation. So you can see how our American born and raised Filipino children may find it difficult to understand these social-cultural traits of Filipinos.

In Philippine society, one who has committed violations of the social code suffers shame. To be ashamed is to suffer a sense of worthlessness and nothingness. Shame is a powerful deterrent to anti-social behavior. This concept is what our American born or raised kids usually do not grasped or fully comprehend. They sometimes ridicule us for being old-fashioned in our behavior or attitude in this society. They think we are behind the times. But social values are not subject to times or conditions.

Folk tales transmit social-cultural values to children as they are growing up.

In America, it seems that kids or even adults have lost their sense of shame for their anti-social behavior. Research studies on social behavior of students indicate that the majority of them do not understand the sense of guilt or shame with their anti-social actions, such as threatening or hitting teachers, petty thievery, or even criminal actions, disrespect in the classroom. An Indication is that they are sometimes allowed to return to their classes with a slight slap on the wrist, so to speak, and behave as if nothing had happened. Their classmates even idolize them as some kind of heroes. Classroom situations have been described as permissive and destructive. Discipline has gone out of the window.

Two Iowa teachers attended a summer workshop at Purdue University. They brought lessons of what they had learned about value clarification. They were seeking ways to counter disrespect in the classroom and to instill understanding that citizenship is a process, not a birthright.

In one of the *Time* magazine issue that I have read, I found an excellent article on raising moral children, how moral intelligence develops in kids. Here is a key quote from the article:

"Moral intelligence isn't only acquired by memorization of rules and regulations, by dint of abstract classroom discussion, or kitchen compliance. We grow morally as a consequence of learning how to be with others, how to behave in this world, a learning prompted by taking to heart what we have seen and heard. The child is an ever attentive witness of grown up morality."

These are words by Psychiatrist and Harvard Professor Robert Coles, author of the Pulitzer prize winning *Children of Crises* and the best selling *The Spiritual Life of Children*, and his new book *The Moral Intelligence of Children*.

4. The fourth and final point is that folk lore elevates society to a higher level of behavior. This is where the parable and folk lore meet perfectly. Jesus sought always to elevate the ethics and behavior of the Gentiles and the Jews through concise and well presented parables. The listeners of these parables, no doubt, came out with a renewed sense of values and were challenged to follow a new path of life. Folk tales have the same effect on the listeners.

Time does not allow me to tell these wonderful folk tales in my book *Tales from the 7,000 Isles*.

So I close with this summary statement. Folk tales are good Christian educational tools, like the parables, in teaching our children and adults some solid truths about faith, hope, and love.

APPENDICES

Lord's Prayer in Cebuano (Visayan)

Amahan namo, nga anaa sa mga langit,
Pagdaygon ang Imong Ngalan.
Moabot kanamo ang Imong gingharian,
Matuman ang Imong pagbuot,
Dinhi sa yuta maingon sa langit.
Ang kalan-on namo sa matag adlaw,
Ihatag kanamo karong adlawa,
Ug pasayloa kami sa among mga sala,
Ingon nga nagapasylo kami sa mga nakasala kanamo,
Ug dili kami itugyan sa mga panulay,
Hinonoa luwasa kami sa dautan.
Kay imo man ang Gingharian,
Ang gahum ug ang himaya
Hangtud sa kahangturan.
Amen.

The Shepherd's Song in Cebuano (Visayan)

Si Jehova mao ang aking magbabantay; Walay makulang kanako.

Siya nagapahigda kanako sa mga sibsibanan mga malunhaw; Siya nagatultol kanako sa daplin sa ma tubig nga malinaw.

Gipalig-on niya ang akong kalag: Ginamandoan niya ako sa mga dalan sa pagkamatarung tungod sa iyang ngalan.

Oo, bisan magalakaw ako latas sa walog sa landong sa kamatayon, Ako walay kahadlok sa bisan unsa nga dautan; Kay Ikaw nagauban kanako: Ang imong baras ug ang imong sungkod, kini nagapalig-on kanako.

Ikaw nagaandam ug pagkaon sa atubangan ko tinambongan sa akong mga kaaway; Gidihog mo ang akong ulo sa lana: Ang akong copa nagaawas.

Sa pagkamatuod ang kaayo ug mga mahigugmaong-kalolot magasunod kanako sa adlaw ngatanan sa akong kinabuhi: Ug sa balay ni Jehova magapuyo ako sa walay katapusan.

The Lord's Prayer—Ama Namin in Tagalog

Ama namin na sa langit ka

Sambahin nawa ang pangalan mo

Dumating nawa ang kaharian mo

Gawin nawa ang iyong kalooban

Kung paano sa langit, gayon din naman sa lupa

Ibigay mo sa amin ngayon ang aming kakanin sa araw araw

At ipatawad mo sa amin ang aming mga utang

Gaya naman namin na nagpagpatawad sa mga may utang sa amin

At huwag mo kaming ihatid sa tukso

Kundi iligtas mo kami sa masama

Sapagkat iyo ang kaharian, at kapangyarihan

At kaluwalhatian, magpakailan man

Siya nawa.

The Lord's Prayer—Amami in Ilocano

Amami nga addaka sadi langit
Madaydayaw kuma ti Naganmo
Umay kuma ti pagariam.
Maaramid kuma ti pagayatam
Kas sadi langit kasta met ditoy daga
Itedmo kadakam ita ti taraonmi iti inaldaw
Ket pakawanen na kami kadagati ut utangmi
A kas met panamakawanmi kadagiti nakautang kadakami
Ket dinakam iyeg iti pannakasulisog
No di ket isalakanna kami iti dakes
Ta kukuam ti pagarian, ti makabalin kenti gloria
Amen.

Psalm 23-Mga Awit 23 in Tagalog

Ang Panginoon ay aking pastor hindi ako mangangailangan

Kaniyang pinahihiga ako sa sariwang pastulan

Pinapatnubayan niya ako sa siping ng mga tubig na pahingahan

Kaniyang pinapananauli ang aking kaluluwa

Pinapatnubayan niya ako sa mga landas ng katuwiran alang alang sa kaniyang pangalan

Oo, bagaman ako'y lumalakad sa libis ng lilim ng kamatayan

Wala akong katatakutang kasamaang sapagka't ikaw ay sumasama sa akin

Ang iyong pamalo at ang iyong tungkod ay nagsisialiw sa akin

Iyong pinaghahandaan ako ng dulang sa harap ko sa harapan ng aking mga kaaway

Iyong pinahiran ang aking ulo ng langis

Ang aking saro ay inaapawan

Tunay na ang kabutihan at kaawaan ay susunod sa akin sa lahat ng mga kaarawan ng aking buhay

At ako'y tatahan sa bahay ng Panginoon magpakailan man.

Psalm 23—Dalit 23 in Ilocano

Ti Apo ti pastorko
Adda aminen a masapulko
Iti nalangto a karuotan, paginnanaenak
Iti sibay dagiti natalna nga ubbog
Iturongnak
Baro a pigsa, ipaayna kaniak

Iturongnak iti tumutop a dalan gapu iti naganna
Uray pay no aglasatak iti ingget sipnget a lugar
Diakto agbuteng ta addaka kaniak
Ti sarukod ken bastommo salaknibandak

Mangisaganaka iti padaya nga agpaay kaniak
Iti imatang dagiti kabusorko
Linanaam ti ulok Ket agliplipias ti tasak
Awan dudua a kumuyogto kaniak ti kinaimbag
Ken ti kinamangayatmo bayat ti panag biagko
Ket agtaengak to nga agnanayon ti balaymo.

GLOSSARY

Abad	Family Clan in Juneau
Alaskeros	Early Filipino settlers in Alaska
Adobo	Popular Filipino dish (pork or chicken)
Aklanons	Also called Antiqueñons from Antique
Aswang	Mythical vampire
Amami	Our father (Ilocano)
Ama Namin	Our Father (Tagalog)
Amahan Namo	Our Father (Cebuano/ Visayan)
Apo Dios	God (Ilocano)
Banal Na Kasulatan	New Testament (Tagalog)
Bisaya	Language In the Visayan Islands
Carillo	Family clan in Juneau
Dalit	Psalm 23 (Ilocano)
Filipino	People of the Philippines
Hilagaynon	Also Ilonggo language
Hiya (He yah)	Shame (Filipino cultural trait)
Ilocano	Language and natives in Northern Luzon provinces

Kababayan	Fellow country men and women, compatroits
Lumpia	Popular Filipino dish (vegetables & ground pork)
Lualhati (Lulu)	Glory (beloved eldest daughter of the Guillermos)
Mabait	Good, kind, respecful
Mga Awit	Psalm 23 (Tagalog)
Nanang	Honorific for Mother (Ilocano)
Naimbag Nga Damag	Good News, New Testament
Pabaon	Food to go
Paksiw	Fish dish
Papaitan	Popular Ilocano dish (goat stew)
Pastor	Honorific for Filipino ministers
Pinakbet	Popular Ilocano dish of vegies and pork
Si Jehovah Mao	Psalm 23 (Bisaya)
Tatang	Honorific for Father (Ilocano)
Tikbalang	Mythical satyr (horse with human features)
Tilapia	Also called Peter's fish
Tinguian	Natives of Abra province
Waray waray	Language in Samar and Leyte provinces
Yadao Family	clan in Juneau

BIBLIOGRAPHY

USEFUL RESOURCES RELEVANT TO THE GENERAL THEME OF WITNESS FOR CHRIST FROM THE LIBRARY OF BEATRICE L. SHEPARD

Arctander, John W. *The Apostle of Alaska. Story of William Duncan of Metlakahtla.* Fleming Revell Co. New York 1980.

Barth. Karl. *Word of God and Word of Man.* Harper Bros. New York 1928.

Beattie, William Gilbert. *Marsden of Alaska. A Modern Indian.* Vantage Press, New York 1955.

Boelter, Francis W. *The Covenant People of God.* Tidings, Nashville 1971.

Barclay, William. *The Gospel of John* Vol. 1 & 2. St. Andrew Press. Edinburgh, England 1956.

_____. *Jesus As They Saw Him.* William B. Eerdmans Publishing Co. Grand Rapids Michigan 1994.

Bro, Marguerite Harmon. *Today Makes a Difference.* Thomas Nelson, New York 1970,

Brown, Robert McAfee. *The Bible Speaks To You.* Westminster Press, Philadelphia 1955.

Cahill, Thomas. *The Gifts of the Jews. How a Tribe of Desert Nomads Changed the Way Everyone Thinks and Feels*. Double Day, New York 1998.

Carter, Nancy A. *Jesus in the Gospel of Matthew "Who do you say I am?"* General Board of Global Ministries, New York 1993.

Cherry, Clinton M. *Beliefs of a United Methodist*. Tidings, Nashville 1969.

Curnock, Nehemiah. *Journal of John Wesley*. Capricorn Books. New York 1980.

Davies, Benjamin. *Baker's Harmony of the Gospels*. King James Version. Baker Book House, Grand Rapids Michigan 1991.

Danuenhaur, Nora & Richard, editors. *Haakusteeyi; Our Culture Tilingit Stories*, Vol. 2. University of Washington Press, Seulaska Heritage Foundation, Alaska 1994.

Grant, Frederick C. *Introduction to New Testament Thought*. Abingdon Press, 1950

Godwin, Frank J. *A Harmony of the Life of St. Paul*. Baker Book House, Grand Rapids Michigan 1951.

Guillermo, Artemio R. Editor. *Churches Aflame. Asian-Americans and United Methodism*. Abingdon, Nashville, 1991.

_____ *Tales from the 7,000 Isles*. Read Me Books Vision Books International, Santa Rosa, CA, 95403, 1996.

Howell, Erle. *Methodism in the Northwest*. Parthenon Press, 1966.

Harkness, Georgia. *A Devotional Treasury From The Early Church*. Abingdon Press 1968.

Hudson, Raymond. *Family Afterall. Story of Jesse Lee Home*. Vol. I. Unalaska.

1889-1925. Hardscratch Press, Walnut Creek, CA. 2007.

Jackson, Sheldon. *Alaska, Missions of the North Pacific Coast*. Dodd Mead, New York 1880.

James, Ron. *Jesus Christ in the Ephesians*. Upper Room, Nashville 1987.

Jones, E. Stanley. *Christ of the Mount*. Abingdon Press, 1931.

Kalas, J. Ellsworth. *Parables of Jesus*. Abingdon Press 1988.

Kepler, Thomas. *Journey Into Faith. Forty Meditations*. Abingdon Press. Nashville, 1954.

Lazell, J. Arthur. *Alaskan Apostle. Life Story of Sheldon Jackson*. Harper Bros. New York 1960.

Lewis, C. S. *Mere Christianity*. MacMillan Co. New York 1956.

Luccock, Halford E. *Communicating the Gospel*. Lyman Beecher Lectures at Yale. Harper Bros. New York 1954.

Middleton, W. Vernon. *Methodism in Alaska and Hawaii*. Parthenon Press 1959.

McEllhenny, John. *United Methodism in America. A Compact History*. Abingdon Press 1992.

Noley, Homer. *First White Frost. Native Americans and United Methodism.* Abingdon Press 1991.

Pelican, Jaroslav. Editor. *Modern Religious Thought.* Little Brown Co. Boston 1990.

Pels, Jacqueline B. *Family Afterall. Alaska's Jesse Lee Home.* Vol. II. Hardscratch Press, 2008.

Ramsay. Paul. *Who Speaks For The Church?* Abingdon Press, 1967.

Roberts, Arthur. *Tomorrow is Growing Old. Stories of the Quakers in Alaska.* Barclay Press, Newberg, Ore.1978.

Roscoe, Stanley N. *From Humboldt to Kodiak 1886-1895.* Baptist Mission of Kodiak Alaska, Limestone Press, Kingston, Ontario 1992.

Shackley, Grant S. *Heritage and Hope. The African-American Presence in United Methodism.* Abingdon Press 1991.

Sano, Roy I. *Ouside the Gate. A Study of the Letter to the Hebrews.* Board of Global Ministries, New York. 1982.

Seifert, Harvey. The Church in the Community Action. Abingdon Press 1952.

Sherwood, Morgan B. *Exploration of Alaska1865-1900.* University of Alaska Press, Fairbanks 1992.

Shepard, Bea & Claudia Kelsey. *Have Gospel Tent Will Travel.* The Methodist Church in Alaska Since 1886. Conference Council on Ministries. Alaska Missionary Conference. 1988.

Schnase, Robert. *Five Practices of Fruitful Congregations*. Abingdon Press 2007.

Scott, Mcknight. *Interpreting the Synoptic Gospels*. Baker Books. 1988.

Stroke, Donald B. *Faith Under Fire. Challenges to the Church In a Changing World*.

Word Books. Waco, Texas 1969.

Ward, William Ralph Jr. *Faith in Action*. Academy Books. Rutland 1986.

Watson, Lillian Eichler. Editor. *Light From Many Lamps. A Treasury of Inspiration*. Simon & Schuster, New York 1990.

Wijk-Bos, Johanna. *Ruth and Esther. Women in Alien Lands*. Abingdon Press 2001.

Tribute to Bea Shepard on her Memorial Service at Douglas Community United Methodist Church. Bea passed away November 1, 2013.

Greetings

We are not here in person but we are with you in spirit and in truth in this memorial service of our dearest and beloved friend Beatrice Shepard. Our friendship started many years ago when we were both members of the General Commission on Archives and History. She was the first Alaskan I ever met. Since I'm an avid historical buff I have been curious about the Alaskan muktuk the famous delicacy of the Tlingits and Yupiks. Unfortunately muktuk was only available to the far northern tribes. Not for sale in Juneau. However, she had a more interesting news for me. There are in Juneau/Douglas area a tribe called Filipinos who are waiting to be ministered for Christ. So with her invitation and the Douglas Church we accepted the challenge of what she proposed as the Filipino Ministry. So for 13 summer months we faithfully came to Douglas and set up an organized program of visitation of our kababayans, fellow Filipino-Americans. Our work was a joy calling on our countrymen and women in their homes and places of work. The program resulted in many Filipinos who had never attended a Protestant worship service and

160

several of them later on took up membership. Some of them are even present in this church to this day. Our ministry which we have written in book form Aurora Borealis is our loving tribute to Bea Shepard. She was a generous steward as she provided the major portion of our maintenance during our ministrations to our benighted kababayans.

This iconic lady Bea Shepard is our model of Christian witnessing. The Methodist faith has been strengthened in Alaska because of Bea's dynamic contribution by her writings and personal witness. Her book "Have Gospel Tent Will Travel" which she co-authored with her devoted friend and companion Claudia Kelsey is the historical testimony of the spread of the Methodist faith in Alaska. We glory with her productive involvement in the work and program of the Alaska Missionary Conference, and particularly in the Douglas Community church. Her handiwork includes the acquisition of the Eagle River Camp which is the site of many of our summer programs. This is foresight of Bea whose vision was to see that the church is buttressed with the resources for a vital Christian presence in the community. She lifted up Christ.

And so Bea, our dearest and beloved friend, we bid you farewell with our deepest love as you rest in peace with our Heavenly Father.

Art & Cora Guillermo

ABOUT THE AUTHORS

Artemio & Corazon Guillermo are retired high school and university teachers. Art taught at the University of Northern Iowa, Bowling Green State University, and Arkansas State University. He obtained his Bachelor of Arts from Silliman University, Philippines, and his M.A. and Ph.D. degrees from Syracuse University. He was a Crusade Scholar of the United Methodist Church and a Fulbright Scholar of the United States/Philippines Educational Foundation. He served as president of the National Association of Filipino/American United Methodists. Art was general editor of *Churches Aflame—Asian-American*

United Methodist Churches—Abingdon Press, and *Historical Dictionary of the Philippines* (3rd edition), Scarecrow Press. Cora earned her Bachelor of Science in Education from Far Eastern University, Philippines, and M.A. from Bowling Green State University. She taught special education in Arkansas public schools and Cedar Falls High School, Iowa. They have four grown handsome daughters and seven magnificent grandchildren.

Aunt Claudia's Dolls, a Museum

Located in the **Triangle Building**
114 South Franklin Street Suite 102
(above Hearthside Books)

Museum Hours
Tuesday - Saturday 11-5
(and by appointment)
FREE Admission

Contacts
auntclaudiasdolls@hotmail.com
(907) 586-4969
Websites
www.auntclaudiasdolls.com
www.maryellenfrank.com

dolls/miniatures

Aunt Claudia's Dolls, a Museum

Aunt Claudia's Doll Museum houses the extensive collection of antique and ethnic dolls and miniatures, from the turn of the century to Alaskan territorial days, left by old time Alaskan, Claudia Kelsey, for the enjoyment of adults and children living in or visiting Juneau, Alaska.

The studio of internationally recognized doll artist Mary Ellen Frank is located in the museum where she is creating her figures while you watch. Her work and collection of Eskimo, Inuit, Native Alaskan, Canadian and Russian dolls are on exhibit.

Welcome to Aunt Claudia's Dolls, a Museum. We house the large collection of dolls belonging to Claudia Kelsey during her lifetime. In addition, doll maker Mary Ellen Frank has her studio in the museum and displays her collections of Northern Native dolls with Claudia's in the revolving collections area.

Our doors can always be opened.
Please call for scheduled hours and other contact information if you need to have the museum opened for your viewing pleasure.
Call (907) 586-4969 for these details.
Aunt Claudia's Dolls, A Museum
114 S. Franklin St., Suite #102
Juneau, Alaska (AK) 99801
(907) 586-4969
auntclaudiasdolls@hotmail.com